Dark forces are at work in the Kingdom of Arkendale. People are disappearing from the border towns, where strange figures move through the hushed streets. Meanwhile, in Helmsgard, wild rumours are starting to spread. But it's only when you peer from your window one cold winter's night that you find out just how close the Shadow has crept...

From this point onwards, you are in control of an epic adventure. Every choice is yours, and your survival depends upon the decisions you make. There are battles to fight and picture clues to unravel as you draw ever closer to one final, fateful choice.

One thing is for certain: as the mysteries of your past are revealed, it becomes clear that it's not just your fate that hangs in the balance – it's the fate of the entire kingdom.

HOW TO PLAY

This book is split into numbered entries. At the end of most entries, you'll be presented with a choice about what to do next. When you've made your choice, turn to that entry. Your adventure begins at entry 1, but after this it will proceed in the order determined by your choices.

LOG BOOK

Turn to the end of these instruction pages to see your Log Book. This is where you'll keep track of all the relevant details of your quest. It's split into the six sections detailed below, and you'll need a pencil to keep them all up-to-date.

Life points

You start with 12 Life points, but lose points if you're hurt. If you drop to 0 you die, and the game ends. At various points you'll be able to heal yourself and regain lost Life points, but **you can never have more than 12 in total.** Each time you gain or lose Life points, update the number in your Log Book.

Abilities

You have four abilities: ATHLETICISM, SIXTH SENSE, ENDURANCE and SKILL. Your starting level for each is 3 points. **Before you start the game, add 1 point to the ability of your choice.** At various moments in your quest, you will gain more Ability points. It's up to you which abilities to upgrade. If you receive more than 1 Ability point at the same time, you can add

SHADOW CHASER

Which path
will YOU take?

Designed by Reuben Barrance
Edited by Sam Taplin

With thanks to Kate Nolan, Tom Taplin, Andy Prentice,
and Darran Stobbart for their careful proofreading.

First published in 2021 by Usborne Publishing Ltd., Usborne House,
83-85 Saffron Hill, London EC1N 8RT, England. usborne.com

Usborne Verlag, Usborne Publishing Ltd., Prüfeninger Str. 20, 93049
Regensburg, Deutschland, VK Nr. 17560

Cover illustration by Christopher Park

Inside illustrations by Tom Knight

Text, cover illustration and inside illustrations
© Usborne Publishing, 2021

The name Usborne and the balloon logo are
trade marks of Usborne Publishing Ltd.

A CIP catalogue record for this book is available from the British Library.

ISBN 978-1-474-96048-9   05270/03   JFMAMJJASO D/21

Printed in Slovakia.

MIX
Paper from
responsible sources
FSC® C022120

Usborne
CHOOSE YOUR OWN STORY

SHADOW CHASER

Simon Tudhope

Illustrated by Tom Knight

them all to the same ability, or spread them across different abilities. You can also lose Ability points, and you must decide which ability to downgrade. Remember to update your Log Book whenever an ability level changes.

Weapons
When you pick up a weapon, write it down in your Log Book. If the weapon has a special ability, make a note of it in the same box.

Armour
When you pick up armour, write it down in your Log Book, and make a note of its defence bonus in the same box.

Items
You will both pick up and lose items on your adventure. Remember to write down any item that you pick up in your Log Book, and delete it if you're instructed to do so. Most items can help you in some way.

Notes
During your quest, you'll see and learn things that could be useful later on. It might be a small detail, or the entry number for a passage you want to refer back to. Whatever it is, you can jot it down in the notes section of your Log Book.

COMBAT

You fight by rolling two dice. Here's an example of what you'll see before combat starts:

GUARD

Rounds: 5

Damage: 3

YOU

The skulls are your opponent's Combat points. The aim is to cross them all out, and you must do this within a certain number of rounds. One skull is one Combat point. The number of rounds you have to defeat your opponent is shown to the left beneath their name.

At the start of each round, you decide how strong an attack to launch against your opponent. You do this by choosing from three options:

Roll 7 or more: your opponent loses 1 Combat point
Roll 9 or more: your opponent loses 3 Combat points
Roll 11 or more: your opponent loses 5 Combat points

Once you've chosen, roll two dice. **Remember, if you choose to roll for '7 or more' but actually roll a 10, you still only score the points for '7 or more'.**

The more Combat points you aim for, the lower your chances of success. But you only have a limited number of rounds in which to cross out all your opponent's Combat points. If you fail to do so, you must turn to the Defeat entry. Remember, defeat does not necessarily mean death.

Every time you fail to match your chosen roll, you must cross out one or more of your Life points. These are the flames beneath your heading. One flame is one Life point. To find out how many to cross out, look at your opponent's Damage rating, which is shown to the right beneath their name. If your Life points are reduced to zero at any point in the combat, you are dead and your adventure is over.

Before the fight starts, check your Log Book to see how many Life points you have. Then turn back to the combat entry, and cross out any flames needed to show the correct amount. Once the fight is over, update your Log Book if you lost any Life points.

During the fight, use your armour bonus after each unsuccessful roll. The bonus is described in the text when you pick up the item.

If you're fighting more than one opponent, you must choose which opponent you want to attack before every roll. You don't have to defeat one opponent before moving on to the next, but you must defeat all your opponents before turning to the Victory entry.

For a step-by-step example of how combat works, turn to the back of the book.

PICTURE PUZZLES

There are twelve picture puzzles, but which ones you encounter will depend on the choices you make on your journey. If you solve a puzzle correctly, it will reveal an entry number to turn to. If you can't solve the puzzle, you'll be given a different entry number. But don't give up too soon, or your quest could come to an unhappy end...

USBORNE QUICKLINKS

If you don't have two dice for the combat, you can use an online dice roller instead. For links to an online dice roller, and also to print out extra copies of the Log Book, go to usborne.com/Quicklinks and enter 'Shadow Chaser', or simply scan the QR code below.

LOG BOOK

LIFE POINTS

12

ABILITIES

SIXTH SENSE	ATHLETICISM
3	3

ENDURANCE	SKILL
3	3

WEAPONS

ARMOUR

ITEMS

NOTES

1

For a moment, you think that you've dreamt it, the cry that tears the night in two and jolts you from your sleep. A hard winter's moon pierces the shutters. Then there's the scrape of metal and a bang at the door. Your hand closes over the locket that you keep beneath your pillow, and you cross the floorboards to peek outside. There are five figures, dressed in dark cloaks with hoods over their heads. The leader raises his gloved fist to strike the door, and then stops, as if sensing something. He looks up and you pull back, but not before catching a glimpse of his face. It's deathly white, and his eyes are sunken and sightless.

"My apologies for waking you, young apprentice," he calls. "But an old friend begs an audience."

His laughter creeps up the walls. You hear that cry again, and realise it's deep inside you. Some forgotten terror. Who is this man that's come calling in the night, and why does he seem so familiar? Add a LOCKET to your LOG BOOK.

If you wish to open the door and ask him yourself, turn to **276**.

If you want to buy some time and call down from the window, turn to **127**.

If you want to escape into the alley behind the workshop, turn to **185**.

2

You'll have to choose whether to fight with FLYNT or the SHADOW BLADE.

If you choose FLYNT, turn to **281**.

If you choose the SHADOW BLADE, turn to **144**.

3

The first firecracker disappears inside the river monster's mouth with a puff of smoke. An icy laugh rolls through the valley and dislodges a small shower of pebbles from the cliffs on either side. Perhaps... As the tentacles wrap themselves around your body, you hurl the rest of the firecrackers high against the cliffs. They explode with a flash and a bang, and the monster looks up in surprise. There's a groaning sound, and before she can react, a large rock falls straight through her face. The tentacle slips from your waist. You leap backwards just in time, as the monster disappears beneath a hail of stone.

Delete the FIRECRACKERS from your LOG BOOK,
gain 1 ABILITY point, then turn to **382**.

4

You grab hold of the tailgate and clamber onto the rear step, but your foot slips and you find yourself being dragged along, clinging to the cart by your fingertips.

If your ENDURANCE level is 5 or higher, turn to **383**.

If it's 4 or lower, turn to **135**.

5

With a sigh of relief you see the sign for the Cat and Coracle, swaying in the breeze. Your memory has not let you down. Without breaking stride you step up to the door and knock softly – the knock that Old Joe taught you. *Rap-a-tap-tap tap rap-tap.* No one stirs. Above your head the sign creaks. The night sky is turning grey and you must be off the streets before dawn. You knock again, as loudly as you dare. A candle flares in a room above, and you hear footsteps on the stairs. You take a deep breath as the bolt draws back, and the door swings open.

Gain 1 ABILITY point, then turn to **212**.

6

You stumble backwards and feel a burning pain. Clutching your side, thinking it must be Pustula's bite, your hand closes over something small and hard and so cold it burns. You reach inside your cloak and take out the blue stone you found in the river. It shines with such a fierce light that you have to look away.

"What's that?" Pustula cries, his decorum forgotten.

You have no idea, but it's burning your palm. With a cry, you fling it down the creature's throat.

Its light fades as it drops deeper and deeper down the cavernous pit. Pustula waits and then laughs.

"Well, that was a pretty trinket."

As you raise Flynt wearily, a tremor runs through Gucifer. A waft of foul air rises, followed by an unearthly scream and a flash that turns everything white. You're thrown backwards out of the creature's mouth and land far out to sea.

Something nudges your side. It's a piece of driftwood. You grab hold, and remember nothing more.

Turn to **255**.

7

You tell her how the mutant beast attacked without warning, and while defending yourself, you snapped the chain around its throat. You say how it turned into a great hound and a bat and they disappeared into the night.

The alchemist stares at you until you begin to doubt your own words. Then she tips her head back and laughs so hard that her single front tooth wobbles in its socket.

"You speak the truth, that's certain – liars look more confident."

She hobbles over to a table at the back of the room.

"He escaped the lab in great pain, the melding wasn't stable. He ran before I could break the chain and separate the two poor creatures once more. You did them a great service..."

Suddenly she looks thoughtful, and rummages about in a drawer under the table.

"Perhaps I can return the favour. If you ever face anyone that uses a magic staff like me, open this."

She drops a small yellow pouch into your hand. It's filled with some kind of powder.

Add a YELLOW POUCH to your LOG BOOK,

and turn to **119**.

8

Your shot hits Hairy Jonas right on his bald head with a satisfying splat. He raises his fists angrily and takes a step towards you. But then he stops and rubs his eyes. His face goes red. He tips back his head and wails like a child.

"What did you do that for?" he cries in pitiful tones.

You turn around in triumph, but something warm and wet splats against your cheek.

"Don't gloat too soon, cockle!"

Karl lowers his gunger and laughs. In fact, the whole crew are laughing. Even Jonas giggles, although he has no idea what everyone finds so funny. Hot tears run down your cheeks.

"I hate you all!" you shout in a high-pitched voice.

Then you run to the far end of the ship and hide behind the nets.

Deduct 1 ABILITY point, then turn to **52**.

9

You come to a crossroads. If you want to go:

North, turn to **333**.   South, turn to **57**.

East, turn to **248**.   West, turn to **204**.

10

"Stop, thief!"

You look up to see the guard running towards you. The driver looks over his shoulder and cries out. With a lash of his reins the cart jolts forward and sends you sprawling onto the road. You barely have time to reach for Flynt before the guard is upon you.

GUARD

Rounds: 4   Damage: 2

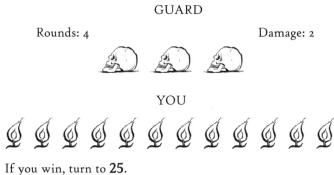

YOU

If you win, turn to **25**.

If you lose, turn to **374**.

11

Seeing the guards, you remember the one you passed just recently, and that feeling of wanting to keep out of sight returns. You hide in a doorway. You've never felt this way about the city guards before. But then you've never been chased through the streets by a group of armed men either. It's understandable that you're wary. You stare

down at your feet. Alerting the guards is the sensible thing to do...
so why the hesitation?

If you decide to carry on to the station, turn to **325**.

If you want to go to the workshop instead, turn to **377**.

If you decide to go to the market, turn to **331**.

12

The sun has risen above the horizon. Looking back towards
Helmsgard, you see its rays glinting off the old Astronomer's
Tower. But your attention is drawn away by strange noises further
down the road. Songs and laughter, low rumbles and metallic
clanking. The road skirts the edge of Gloamwold Forest. Who could
be moving so cheerfully past that sinister place? Then the cart
rounds the bend and the answer is revealed. The circus is coming to
town! The ringmaster rides up front, wearing a red waistcoat that
strains against its big gold buttons, and a blue top hat studded with
stars. At the sight of your cart he raises a hand and cries:
"Company... HALT!"

Your driver pulls his horses up fast and yells: "Get off the road you thieving vagabonds, can't you see we're in a hurry? Nobody wants your sort in town anyway!"

The ringmaster's stare hardens.

"Harley, Barley, Cob, you're needed outside, boys!"

The cart behind him shudders. The door swings open and three of the biggest men you've ever seen emerge.

"Now wait just a minute," your driver stammers. "I was only joking around. Of course you folks are welcome here. As a matter of fact I..."

His voice trails off as the three circus giants loom over him.

If you want to leap from the cart and call for help,

turn to **166**.

If you don't, turn to **352**.

13

You leap backwards as a spiked metal ball whistles past your nose. A guard steps out from behind a statue, dressed all in black. She must have heard your footsteps and lain in wait. The ball is on the end of a chain that's wrapped around her wrist.

"Who approaches the Temple of the Shadow?"

You ask if she always attacks first and asks questions later.

"My task is to guard the Temple, nothing more."

She advances, whirling the deadly chain above her head.

Turn to **264**.

14

You toss the bow aside and fumble for Flynt, but the man is already upon you. Down the street, you see Madoc stepping over his opponent and running in your direction. He's shouting... but everything has gone strangely quiet. As you fall, you let out a sigh. Your adventure is over.

15

A sign on the door of the Weeping Willow proclaims 'Traders drink half price', and it sounds like they're taking full advantage of the offer. The noise and heat hit you as you step inside. A large fire burns at the back of the room and the floor is covered with sawdust and beer. The traders sit around a long table, wearing their trader numbers around their necks for their half-price drinks. A group of off-duty guards are standing by the bar. You'll have to be careful not to draw attention to yourself – if you walk up to the wrong trader and they call out to Madoc, the guards will almost certainly notice. So you'll have to work out for yourself which is the mapmaker.

Turn over, and when you think you've spotted who it is, add up the numbers on the tags of all the **other** traders, and turn to that entry.

If you can't find the mapmaker, turn to **138**.

16

Suddenly you see the pictures in the margins. You trace the route from the rising sun on the right to the setting sun on the left, then up to the full moon, then down to the flame burning underground. The lines make a cross over a tree with a strange symbol on its trunk. Gain 1 ABILITY point.

Madoc peers closely and gasps.

Turn to **254**.

17

You scramble up the slope onto a rocky ridge. The wind howls and swirls and knifes through your clothing until your hands and feet are numb. Down below, you can see the galley moored to a dock that's cut into a grey cliff face. There's no one to be seen, and you begin your descent.

If you have a ROPE WITH HOOK and want to use it, turn to **298**.

If you don't, roll one DICE and add it to your ENDURANCE level.

If your total is 10 or higher, turn to **214**.

If it's 9 or lower, turn to **370**.

18

Maybe it's the twitch your left eye suddenly develops, maybe it's the instincts Owen acquired in his long hours on watch at the East gate, but something about your blank stare doesn't convince. You feel a palm on your chest.

"Hello, Rowan. Haven't seen you in a while."

You try to keep your voice as flat as his, but there's a catch in your throat when you tell him you fell ill. It sounds hollow in your ears.

"Could you step into the light, please, Rowan?"

You look at him with pleading eyes, but Owen's expression doesn't change. You have no choice but to reach for Flynt.

OWEN THE GATEKEEPER

Rounds: 5   Damage: 2

YOU

If you win, turn to **260**.

If you lose, turn to **128**.

19

Your brother sinks to the chamber floor. His face flickers into view and it looks lonely and scared.

"My name's Ash, by the way."

He tries to laugh, but it ends with a choke.

"You never asked."

And then his shadow veils his face for the last time, and he dies.

Turn to **207**.

You tell her everything that's happened since you were awoken so suddenly in the night. She sits cross-legged on the mossy ground, her chin cupped in her hands, and stays that way long after you've finished your story. High above, a crow caws. You clear your throat and she stirs.

"Tell me, sweetie. Did you happen to see the boy's shadow, I wonder, before he died?"

You ask her what she means.

"Oh, don't take no notice of me, my love. Silly rumours reach those whose ears are closer to the ground."

She smiles and leaps to her feet.

"The name's Nettle, by the way, and you're lost, yes? Well, I can show you the way out of here. The only other choice..."

Her voice tails off and you beg her to finish what she was going to say.

"Well, you could try to find the Old Lady of the Forest. She doesn't take kindly to strangers, but she sees and hears all that happens in these parts. If anyone can make sense of your story, it's her. Whether she'd want to..."

She grins and shrugs.

If you'd like to search for the Old Lady of the Forest,
turn to **219**.

If you'd like to get back to Helmsgard as quickly as possible,
turn to **421**.

21

"I was wrong. Your mother would never have entrusted the location of the Flame to such a fool."

His disappointment turns to anger.

"Back to the temple, carpenter's apprentice."

You wake to find yourself strapped to the Dial. Its markings light up and start to rotate. Something flashes across the disc, and darkness descends. Your adventure is over.

22

Your knuckles turn white as you dig your nails into your palms, but you stay where you are. Old Joe wanted to turn you in. Your own father and the most steadfast, dependable man you know. So what hope is there of finding help in this city of drones? Your only chance is to stay hidden until you have a plan.

The innkeeper nods slightly and winks. There's more strength in that gesture than in the mightiest blow. You watch the wagon rumble past and down the road. In the distance, the Black Tower looms over The Tangles. It has no turrets and no parapets. No light glints off its walls. It's like a doorway into darkness. The hairs rise on the back of your neck as you turn away.

Turn to **113**.

23

A crowd has gathered to watch you wrestle the urchin. He's surprisingly strong, and you have to bang his head against the ground to finally stop him squirming. You take back the bracelet, and he sits up and touches his temple with a wince. As you turn to leave, a group of youths point at him and laugh.

Add a SILVER BRACELET to your LOG BOOK,

then turn to **344**.

24

There – that must be the square! You leap as the beast rears and scrapes and tries to pull its great weight up before the ground disappears beneath it. But it's too late. The Sentinels lift their orbs, and each one shoots bolts of lightning in eight directions at once. They flash past you on all sides as the dragon screams, and falls silent at last. You're safe.

Gain 1 ABILITY point.

As smoke curls from its clenched jaws, you watch closely for any movement. You haven't forgotten that voice either, but no rider emerges from under the charred wings.

Finally, you look around. Pale light streams through stained glass windows and ripples across the floor. Outside, the dark shape of a fish glides slowly past. On the back wall, you see a stone door. The faint outline of a flame shimmers on its surface. Cautiously, you put one foot into the next square, but the Sentinels' orbs stay clasped to their chests. They don't wake for the Guardian.

Striding across, you push against the door with all your might. The outline of the flame blazes and you remember what you were told – only the Guardian can open the door to the chamber. The stone slab starts to rise. You crouch down and peer inside. But as you do, something dark snakes past your foot. Darker even than the passage beyond. A purple light flares, then a familiar voice whispers:

"Come in, Rowan. Don't be scared."

Turn to **376**.

25

Gasping for breath, you look around you. The cart has disappeared and no one's in sight, but it won't be long before the driver alerts the authorities. You drag the guard's body into a side street and make for the old docks.

Turn to **187**.

26

Your brother sinks to the chamber floor. His face flickers into view and he looks lonely and scared.

"My name's Ash, by the way."

He tries to laugh, but it ends with a choke.

"You never asked."

And then his shadow veils his face for the last time.

You bow your head, and are about to turn away when you see his shadow rising up from the ground. Too late you realise your mistake – you've only killed the body. Taking a step back, you fumble for your SHADOW BLADE.

ASH'S SHADOW

Rounds: 4   Damage: 4

YOU

Remember, you can only use a defence bonus if you have the CHAINMAIL VEST, but Ash's shadow can't use his staff.

If you win, turn to **319**.

If you lose, turn to **63**.

27

The 'arm' you're clinging to bends beneath your weight until you're face to face with the lifeless lure. With the last of your strength you reach down with one hand and pull the rope with the hook from your satchel. You'll only have one shot at this. You swing the hook around and let go. It streaks for the trees as the lure slips from your grasp and you pray that it catches on something, anything that can hold your weight. The rope stops and you grab hard...

Roll one DICE and add it to your SKILL level.

If your total is 9 or higher, turn to **420**.

If it's 8 or lower, turn to **362**.

28

You come to a crossroads. If you want to go:

North, turn to **108**.   South, turn to **320**.

East, turn to **9**.   West, turn to **131**.

29

"Protect the child!" yells the ringmaster as half-Harlan leaps from the cart.

One of the circus giants catches him by the ankles and hurls him towards the oncoming kidnappers, but their pale leader holds up his hand and somehow deflects him away without even touching him. He lands in a heap by the forest's edge, and his weapon clatters to the ground near your feet. As the two sides clash, an acrobat flips gracefully over the cart and cuts your bonds.

"Run for the forest, little one!" she whispers. "Quick!"

Grabbing the weapon, you keep low and have almost gained the trees when someone steps in your path. It's your captor. You yell at him to get out of your way – he's unarmed.

"I can't let you go," he replies quietly, and takes a step towards you.

You have no choice but to fight.

Add half-Harlan's weapon, FLYNT, to your LOG BOOK.

Rounds: 3   Damage: 1

YOU

If you win, turn to **66**.

If you lose, turn to **137**.

30

You pull the net from your bag and fling it towards the six marsh goblins.

Delete the NET from your LOG BOOK, then roll one DICE. The number you roll is the number of goblins you snare.

If you roll 1-4, make a note of how many goblins are left, and turn to **198**.

If you roll 5, turn to **356**.

If you roll 6, turn to **228**.

31

The imp shakes her head and sighs as you struggle against your bonds.

"I definitely wouldn't have done that," she says, almost to herself. "Even if I *were* you."

The roots tighten once more and draw you closer to the trunk of the tree. Closer to the round knots that sprout from its bark like boils. And in each knot you see a face, a wooden carving of despair.

You open your mouth but a root stifles your scream. Soon, you too will be just another lump on the trunk of Old Man Tree.

32

You edge down the tunnel and peer around the bend. There are two men, one with his back to you, the other standing to attention. You flatten yourself against the wall. That long, white hair, hanging lank over the cloak... It must be him, surely? You hold your breath to hear what he has to say.

"And the Dial – is it ready?"

"It is, Lord Creeval."

"Then bring the first prisoner. We'll begin shortly."

The guard snaps his heels to attention and disappears down a side passage.

Creeval bows his head before turning abruptly and walking in your direction. Fortunately, he's lost in thought, and you're in the shadows.

If you'd like to follow him, turn to **313**.

If you'd like to follow the guard, turn to **91**.

33

Gain 1 ABILITY point.

Your mind races. You tell the creature that you have no particular interest in the Lonely Isle itself, but you've heard that the Great Speckled Phandrake has chosen this site to nest.

"You may be aware," you add, "that the Great Speckled Phandrake nests only once a generation."

"Indeed? I did not know that. It is always fascinating to learn more of the upper world. Many of our clients seem strangely uncommunicative, and besides, Gucifer takes less of an interest in these matters. Which reminds me..."

Pustula sighs.

"This is most unfortunate once again. We were tasked with intercepting a Rowan of Helmsgard, but so far have rendered our services only to a merchant from Dunbar, a glass-blower from Herikassa and a young woman who sought the world's edge."

"Rendered your services?" Turn to **191**.

"Who gave you this task?" Turn to **390**.

34

Creeval's eyebrows rise as you move your unicorn. It's a suicidal move, in terms of the game.

"I hope you've made your decision, Rowan."

He reaches forwards, when something strange happens. Your pieces start to shudder. Thin lines of flame move out from your Guardian to trace the symbol you've made. It's the symbol you saw on the ship's sail in *Tales of Old*, in the alchemist's chamber, on Hairy Jonas's arm, and other places over the span of your quest.

Creeval stumbles away from the table.

"What have you done?" he hisses.

Thick fog rises in front of your eyes, and as the room fades, you see shadows sliding under the windows. From somewhere in the distance, you hear him cry out.

"Argh, stay back! You work for me! Please, no..."

His scream dies away, and a woman appears out of the fog. She has short, dark hair and wears a yellow robe.

"Rowan, take this."

You look down and see Creeval's dagger in your hands.

"He took it from me, but now it's yours."

Already, she's fading. Her voice is faint.

"A moment more, and all would have been lost..."

The words catch in her throat, and suddenly you know who she is.

"Wait!" you cry. "Don't go!"

"You must go home, Rowan. But remember..." Her voice is a whisper. A mother's whisper in your ear.

"I chose you."

Add the SHADOW BLADE to your LOG BOOK, and make a note that it allows you to fight shadow wraiths, but does not increase the effect of a successful roll against them. For all other combat, use FLYNT.

Gain 1 ABILITY point, then turn to **360**.

35

Despite the figure's cries for help, you decide you haven't got time to waste.

Turn to **157**.

36

Six men surround you. Three of them are dressed like the hooded strangers you've already met, and the rest are city guards. They must be working together! One of the guards starts to chuckle. He reaches for his weapon, but suddenly his chuckle splutters. He looks down to see an arrowhead sticking from his throat.

"Get down!" Madoc shouts.

Another man drops before they realise what's happening. One of the hooded strangers drags you towards the workshop.

"Kill the archer!" he shouts.

You're pulled inside, but desperation makes you strong. You twist from his grasp and reach for Flynt.

HOODED FIGURE

Rounds: 6   Damage: 2

YOU

If you win, turn to **159**.

If you lose, turn to **221**.

37

Creeval sighs.

If you also got the previous question wrong, turn to **21**.

If you answered the previous question correctly, turn to **310**.

38

For each creature, roll one DICE.

If you roll a 2, 4 or 6, Wowl snaps around and snags a wing in his jaws. He shakes the creature like a rag doll and lets it tumble screeching to earth.

If you roll a 1, 3 or 5, the creature dips under Wowl's jaws and sinks its long, hooked beak into his throat.

If all three creatures are killed before Wowl is bitten three times, turn to **139**.

If Wowl is bitten three times, turn to **41**.

39

You tell Madoc that you need to go back to the workshop.

"The message is only one part," you say. "We need the book... I'm sure that's what she means."

"A book from the workshop?"

You nod.

"Then we must hurry. The place may already be under watch."

Together, you make your way back through Helmsgard. The flickering light of the lamps shines on the wet cobbles, but it has stopped raining.

"How are you with a bow and arrow?" Madoc asks.

You say you've had some basic training.

"Then we have a choice. If the workshop is being watched, we want to draw them out. One of us must be the decoy, and one the archer."

In silence, you creep down the street that leads to your home. You crouch behind a barrel, and from there you can see the damage:

the door is hanging on its hinges and a window has been smashed. Madoc sweeps back his cloak to reveal a bow and a quiver of arrows.

"We must hope they didn't know what they were looking for. Listen, if they're here, they'll be waiting inside the workshop. The decoy must draw them outside, where the archer can bring them down."

If you want to be the decoy, turn to **288**.

If you want to be the archer, turn to **167**.

40

The man fights in silence. It's only when Flynt finds its mark that he shows any kind of emotion. He sighs and seems to relax as he sinks to the ground. It looks almost like relief. You turn to see the boy glaring at you. His opponent is dead.

"Didn't I tell you not to go that way? I should have left you to it."

Your eyes widen in recognition.

"Casper?"

"How did you... Rowan?"

You open your mouth to speak, but he holds up a hand.

"Wait. First we get off the streets, then we talk."

He leads you down to the docks and onto a large fishing trawler. Turn to **305**.

41

A soft moan escapes Wowl's clenched teeth. The beating of his wings weakens. The hideous creature screeches in triumph and circles above you.

"Come on, boy," you plead, stroking his soft fur, hugging his neck. But his golden eyes roll back in their sockets. For a long moment they look at you sadly, and then they close.

Together, you fall to earth.

42

The sound of pounding feet reverberates down the narrow alley. Four of the hooded figures are giving chase. The moon is hidden behind the rooftops, but you know these back ways well. At the end of the alley you vault a fence and land in a small yard. A hog is sleeping in a bed of hay. That gives you an idea.

If you'd like to wake the hog by giving it a quick kick as you pass, turn to **143**.

If you'd prefer to carry on your way without waking the hog, turn to **249**.

43

Keeping to the shaded side of the street, you set off for Madoc's cottage on the edge of the city. The street looks tidier than you remember. Cracked cobbles have been replaced and the disused mill that was covered in graffiti has been knocked down. In its place is a statue. You stop dead. Lester Griblin? Is that who's in charge now? He's lost some weight under the chisel, but it's definitely him. His face is turned towards the future, his jaw set firm, and on the plinth are the words: *Free from the Shadow of Doubt.*

You hear footsteps coming down the street, and continue on your way. Soon, you reach a junction.

If you'd like to take the fastest route along the main street, turn to **337**.

If you'd prefer to stick to the side streets, turn to **224**.

44

Suddenly, everyone's attention is drawn to the sound of hooves thundering down the road. The rest of the kidnappers are riding up fast, weapons in hand! Their pale leader is out front, hood blown back, revealing long strands of white, lank hair trailing from his scalp.

Turn to **29**.

45

The crew rush forward to help him down from the Dial.

"Careful, Casper!" says Hairy Jonas. "Don't go breaking your neck now!"

He slaps him on the back so hard he almost knocks him over.

"Got you to do that for me," Casper winces, and Captain Hamshanks roars with laughter.

Then Creeval speaks in a soft voice that somehow fills the cavern.

"My guards will escort you all to the surface, where your ship is anchored in the neighbouring cove."

Your head snaps around in surprise, but he continues.

"I advise you to forget about your friend. You cannot help. The sun is already low in the sky. If I do not see you offshore by the time it sets, Rowan will suffer the fate that was reserved for you. All of you will."

Casper looks up, but Captain Hamshanks puts a hand on his shoulder.

"Find a way," Casper calls in a fierce, choked voice. "Like we always did."

Turn to **160**.

46

Thinking there must be some mistake, you walk up to the guard, determined to clear your name. He looks at you in surprise as you tell him what's happened.

"You'd better come down to the station," he says. "To straighten things out."

Was that a smile flickering across his lips?

Turn to **325**.

You remember entering The Tangles early one morning with Old Joe, and seeing a witch on a broomstick, pointing your way down the street. As the sun rose above the rooftops, you were suddenly blinded by the light from the top of a tower. You turned off, and fought your way against herds of cattle being driven to market. In the end you both gave up, and turned off at a crossroads. The smell of freshly-baked bread wafted towards you on the breeze, and you reached a square where a man was whistling 'Walking on Air' while tying a rope. Leaving the square, you followed Poor Man's Crescent until you finally reached the inn, with the clangs of an anvil coming from a blacksmith's nearby.

If you've followed your memories correctly, you can get to the inn by turning to the number that your finger has traced. If you can't find the route, turn to **89.**

48

There's no chance of escape – you've seen how quickly those things move. Then suddenly the mirror you packed at Madoc's flashes through your mind. You're not sure how it will help, but the shadow is already halfway through the hatch and you're out of ideas. You hold it up, and something strange happens. The mirror seems to trap it, somehow. You feel the shadow's icy cold and see the glass frosting over. Before it destroys the reflection entirely, you force the shadow back through the hole and manage to slam the hatch shut.

Leaning against the wall, you take a moment to regain your breath. Then you leave the chamber and make your way back to the junction.

Gain 1 ABILITY point, then turn to **165**.

49

The ring glows even brighter, then turns to dust on your finger. It's saved you for the last time.

Delete the SILVER RING from your LOG BOOK, then turn back to the **previous entry**.

50

You watch in horror as your captor strikes. The acrobat's mouth drops open, and she falls towards you with frozen surprise in her eyes. You try to scramble away but get tangled up in her arms. Your captor thrusts again and catches you across the shoulder. You manage to leap from the cart, and as blood darkens your tunic you call out for help, yelling that you've been kidnapped.

Deduct 2 LIFE points and turn to **44**.

"The tools because he's a carpenter," you say quietly. "The anchor pendant because he keeps it beneath his pillow, and the violin because that's the instrument he plays."

The other cards sink beneath the surface as the lady holds her hands over the water. Slowly, the three cards you picked start to move. Around and around, faster and faster, until soon they're just a blur around the edge of a whirlpool that disappears down into darkness.

"Home is on the other side," the woman says. "Well done, Rowan."

Gain 1 ABILITY point.

She smiles for the first time

"Who are you?" you ask again.

Her breath catches in her throat.

"I'm your mother."

You stand where you are. You ask her what you're supposed to say.

"I never knew you," you shout.

Her eyes are bright with tears.

"That's why the pool will take you back to Helmsgard."

She takes a deep breath.

"I can only help you this once. We have moments left. The shadows, Rowan. You've seen them. Perhaps you've guessed where they come from. But you don't know what they are. Listen. There's an old king with white eyes and white hair."

"Creeval?" you say, forcing yourself to focus. "He tried to kidnap me."

"He was following orders. He would have taken you to his fortress and split you in two. Split your body from your shadow so you were no longer a threat."

The words tumble out, one over the other, as the garden starts to fade around you.

"Your shadow is what makes you who you are, Rowan. Every free thought and flash of inspiration, every moment of anger and rebellion. It all comes from your shadow. Without it your body is just a slave. You must have seen them? The shadowless people who live but are dead inside. Puppets for the Shadow Reaper."

"Like Creeval?" Turn to **222**.

"Like Odan Britches?" Turn to **404**.

52

Shiverin' Shaun boils up a fish stew laced with rum and spice.

"Th-th-this'll k-k-keep 'ee warm," he says, handing you a bowl filled to the brim.

It does. Casper tips back his head and laughs when he sees your eyes streaming. Add 4 LIFE points.

After dinner, he takes you to the bow of the ship and points to a grey shape on the horizon.

"There's the Lonely Isle," he says. "We should pass it before sunset."

He leans on the gunwale.

"Listen, I've spoken with the captain and I'm going with you."

You look over quickly.

"What about your pay?"

"I've got a bit put by. You seem serious about this, and I've seen enough myself... What's the point of money if there's nothing to go home to? That's all."

You follow his gaze and look out towards the jagged shard of rock.

"OK," you say. "Thanks."

He smiles and claps you on the shoulder.

"Good. That's decided, then. I thought you might play the lonely hero on me."

He strikes a heroic pose, but your laughter is interrupted by a cry from the stern.

Turn to **227**.

53

With a deft flick, your opponent hooks the hatchet from your grasp and sends it clattering across the cobbles. All hope is gone. He backs you up against the wall, defenceless. Soon, his companions arrive, and you're bound, gagged and carried away through the silent streets.

Delete the HATCHET from your LOG BOOK, then turn to **94**.

54

Your aim is true. The goblin screams and falls face-first into a pool of stagnant water.

Deduct 1 ARROW from your LOG BOOK, gain 1 ABILITY point, then turn to **157**.

55

By the time you get to the market many of the traders have left and the rest are packing up. A baker tosses you a pie that was destined for the pigsty. Add 2 LIFE points. Wiping gravy from your chin, you notice a burly guard making enquiries. Your name is mentioned. You've been spotted in the area and are wanted for questioning.

If you'd like to speak to the guard to explain the situation, turn to **46**.

If you want to avoid the guard, and have picked up a HOODED CLOAK, turn to **395**.

If you want to avoid the guard, but don't have a hooded cloak, turn to **273**.

56

You leap for the clothesline, and with surprising grace grasp it neatly and swing to the floor. You can't resist a glance around to see if anyone saw your impressive escape. Someone did – a hooded figure at the end of the alley! You sprint in the opposite direction, and hear that voice again, faint but mocking as it floats over the rooftops.

"All roads lead to us, little Rowan. All of them."

Turn to **42**.

57

You hear a squeak and feel a sudden pain on your calf – you've been bitten by a rat. Deduct 1 LIFE point. Then you come to a crossroads. If you want to go:

North, turn to **306**.   South, turn to **397**.

East, turn to **248**.   West, turn to **204**.

58

You beat your fists against the tree. It stands still and dark in the moonlight. Perhaps you should walk along the line of its reflection? The poem did mention reflection...

You gasp as you walk into the freezing lake. It takes a moment for you to realise that it's not just water you feel, but two long arms, pale as death, dragging you into their icy embrace.

The water closes over your desperate cries. The lake has kept its secret, and your quest is over.

59

You hand her the flask nervously. She snatches it away, dips in a finger and brings a drop to her mouth. Under the light of the lamp, her eyes are almost lost in shadow. She turns abruptly and hobbles from the chamber. Despite her age, you have to hurry to keep up.

"Did I get it wrong?" you ask, emerging back into the laboratory.

"No!" she says, without turning around.

Gain 1 ABILITY point and turn to **365**.

60

By the junction where the river path meets the road a mulberry tree is growing. You stop to pick handfuls of its sweet, black fruit. Add 3 LIFE points.

A child's doll drifts slowly past, and as you watch, you notice a group of people hurrying along the path towards you. Another group appears over the brow of the road. Wiping the juice from your chin, you turn and run. They've found you!

The entrance to the sewers lies just up ahead, in the passageway between two storehouses. You clamber down and wade through thick water and rotten driftwood. Behind you, the sound of boots on rungs echoes between the walls. At the far end, another ladder leads up to the iron grating. You wrench the grating loose and it lands with a dull splash... but you don't hear it. You don't even move. Because the alchemist's cane lies at the entrance to the sewers – and it's broken in two. They found her.

A familiar voice calls out.

"It's over, Rowan. Why don't you come down?"

There's a pleading edge to Old Joe's words. You see his face in the crowd and it's pale and clammy; hollow-eyed, as if in a nightmare.

All the energy drains from your body. You could scramble into the sewers, maybe evade them for a time... but what would be the use? There's nowhere left to run.

Joe pushes through and grips the ladder. You hear his heavy, ragged breathing. And beneath it something else. A growl, coming from the sewer... getting louder. You turn to see two golden eyes emerging from the darkness. You're hit full in the chest and the sky flips over. Joe holds out his hands, but a pair of huge jaws clamps around your waist, and you're borne aloft by a great, black wolf with wings. It's Wowl! He tosses you onto his back with a snarl, and you bury your face in his fur.

When you look up, you're skimming over the roofs of Helmsgard. On either side, the two huge wings rise and fall in silence. You see a red chain around Wowl's neck, and there's a scroll tied to it. Unrolling the parchment, you hold it tight against the whipping wind. Inside is a note, scrawled in a hasty hand.

Turn to **171**, and remember that now you're above the streets, if you were rolling two DICE after every entry, you no longer need to.

61

With a squeal, the marsh goblin disappears into the long grass, his angry chatter growing fainter and fainter.

Turn to **157**.

62

Your arrow misses its target. Deduct 1 ABILITY point.

Luckily, it strikes the iron bars of the cell and not anyone inside.

Delete one ARROW from your LOG BOOK, then turn to **252**.

63

The icy fingers of your brother's shadow reach into your chest. With a hiss of delight, it finds your heart and stops it beating.

64

Casper takes you up on deck to see a mountainous woman with fiery red hair and a sea-serpent tattoo coiled around her neck. She's wearing a jumper that looks like it was woven from hedgehog spines. Her name is Captain Hamshanks.

She leans down and squints in your face. Her breath smells of rum and tobacco.

"I can take you to the Lonely Isle," she says. "But what do you want with that god-forsaken rock?"

If you want to tell her, turn to **339**.

If you want to keep that information to yourself, turn to **150**.

65

You reach for Flynt. The goblin takes one look and disappears into the long grass, his angry chatter growing fainter and fainter.

Turn to **157**.

66

Your captor sighs as he falls to the floor.

"It's better," he whispers.

You step back as he puts his hand inside his tunic, but it emerges with a small, white flower.

"Please, take this. It only grows near my town, far away from here. Wear it, and if you meet half-Harlan, give it to him."

"I thought you were half-Harlan?" you say.

He smiles sadly.

"There were two halves to Harlan."

His eyes close. Taking the flower, you run for the forest.

Turn to **317** and add a WHITE FLOWER to your LOG BOOK.

67

You dash across to the stables. The gate is old and worm-eaten, and the planks groan loudly under your weight. Wincing at the noise, you scramble over – but was it in time? You hear boots on the street.

They're getting louder. Retreating to the farthest corner of the yard, you crouch in an empty stall. But you're only delaying the inevitable. The old gate groans once more as one of your pursuers climbs over and unbars it from the inside. Four dark hoods loom against the night sky.

"What do you want?" you cry.

There's no reply.

"Who are you?" you try again.

One of the figures steps forward, still silent, and reveals the hilt of their weapon.

If you decide to fight these four armed figures, turn to **230**.

If you conclude that the odds are stacked too far against you, turn to **107**.

68

A smile breaks out across your brother's face, before it's veiled once more by shadow.

"Thank you," he says, in a soft voice. "My name is Ash."

Together you leave the chamber and pour the contents of the flask into the ocean. One of the creatures with giant, bat-like wings appears over the horizon and flies you to the Black Tower.

The next day, you have Old Joe brought before you, and tell him that he'll never have to work again. He thanks you, and seems not to notice a single tear running down his cheek.

As your brother's right-hand man, you work hard to soften his rule and redirect his cracked genius. But one morning, you look out over Helmsgard and realise how little good you've done. Gloamwold has been cut to stumps, the air is choked with fumes from the factories, the people are slaves.

You confront your brother, and leave his throne room sure that this time you've gotten through to him. Then your thoughts turn to the old manor house he's just promised you, as thanks for all your good advice.

Maybe he's not so bad after all...

69

After the crush of the high street, it feels strange to have the road to yourself. It makes you uneasy. Hunching your shoulders, you quicken your pace. Your mind wanders to Old Joe, and you smile as you imagine him back in the workshop, bent over a lathe, grunting his greeting without looking up. Pain brings you back to reality. A stabbing pain in your back. Spinning around, you see Woad Griblin. He's the loathsome son of Lester Griblin – chief of the City Guard. He stands there grinning, with a strange-looking weapon in his hand. It's the size of a hammer, with a head like a pickaxe. He takes a step back, pulls a second one from his belt, and weaves them through the air in a complex pattern that's clearly supposed to impress. You smirk as he drops one to the floor. The two of you have never got on. In fact, Woad doesn't like anyone from the Craftsmen's Quarter. More than once he's taunted you for building the bed he sleeps on.

But that doesn't explain why he's attacked you. He sees your confusion.

"Poor 'prentice rat. You have no idea what's going on, do you? But soon you will!"

Deduct 2 LIFE points.

WOAD GRIBLIN

Rounds: 4   Damage: 2

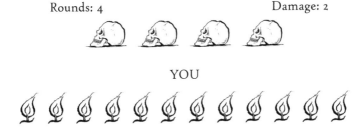

YOU

Unknown to you, each war hammer is coated in poison. If Woad wins four rounds, deduct the damage and go straight to the defeat entry.

If you win, turn to **153**.

If you lose, turn to **182**.

70

With a sigh of relief you run towards Nettle and ask if you're nearly there. She smiles, but there's something about her smile that doesn't look right. It makes her look older, somehow.

"Nearly where, child?"

She laughs, and the sound stops you in your tracks.

"*I'm everywhere.*"

The voice is hard and cold... and *old*.

Suddenly you see what you missed. The path you're running down, the caves in the rock face next to Nettle – they form the image of a skull! The Old Lady has played her game, and you have lost. Nettle disappears, she was never there, and the ground opens up and swallows you whole.

Your only chance of survival is to scramble up the roots before you're buried alive.

Roll one DICE three times. After every roll, add your ENDURANCE level. For each roll under 8, deduct 2 LIFE points.

If you survive, turn to **121**.

71

The lid squeals horribly on its nails and you duck behind the crate. Your heart thumps painfully but the cart continues at the same steady pace. Peering over, you see the driver staring straight ahead. You stick the crowbar back under the lid and wait for the cart to go over a bump in the road before pushing down hard. The clattering of the wheels masks the sound, and the lid lifts open. Inside are bows and arrows.

If you don't already have a BOW, add it to your LOG BOOK, along with 12 ARROWS. If you do, take as many arrows as you need to have 12.

You're about to move on to the next crate when you see a guard walking down the road.

If you'd like to try to open the next crate anyway,

turn to **280**.

If you want to leap from the cart to avoid the guard,

turn to **187**.

72

The last man is nearly upon you. He leaps with his axe raised, ready to bring it down in a cold, grey arc. The look on his face is strangely calm... and doesn't change even when your arrow finds its target. His momentum carries him to your feet, where he stays. You look up to see Madoc running over.

"You did well," he says grimly. "I did not expect them to send six men to ambush one child. You have their respect, Rowan."

You offer him the bow and he claps you on the shoulder.

"Keep it – you may need it again. And we must hurry. The night is quiet and we were loud. Reinforcements could be on their way."

Add a BOW and any remaining ARROWS to your LOG BOOK, then turn to **193**.

73

As you scramble down you send loose rocks bounding and tumbling into the dark, fast-flowing river. But you reach the bottom without falling and set off in the direction of the town. The valley soon narrows, and you're forced to trample through the shallow water. Suddenly you hear a voice close by. It's a woman's voice, ice cold but soft.

"Do you miiind? Dirty boots churning and turning me all to mud. No thought for my sparkle, no. Impure. Impurrre."

You stop and look about you, but there's no one there.

"But you can hear me," says the voice. "Why? Ahhh... yesss..."

A tendril of icy water starts to creep up the back of your leg and you leap forward with a cry.

"That flask, filled with me, and not me. Tears from the Teer. But what have you done? Mixed me, changed me, given me power. I can feeeel it. Pour it into me now, and I will let you pass."

The water swirls around your feet, moving against the current, brushing past your legs like a serpent. This river must be the Teer, one of the rivers used to make the fuel in your flask! Somehow the fuel has brought it to life.

You look around. The valley sides press in, too steep to climb. The quickest way out is back the way you came, but further downstream the valley opens up again.

If you'd like to make a run for it downstream, turn to **394**.

If you'd like to go back the way you came, turn to **361**.

If you'd like to pour the fuel into the river, as she asked, turn to **405**.

74

Joe still has hold of your wrist, but your other arm is free. You reach into the bag and grab the cuffs.

If your SKILL level is 8 or higher, turn to **146**.

If it's 7 or lower, turn to **99**.

75

Crossing the plain, you pass a low outcrop of weathered rocks. Pebbles trickle down onto the path behind and you spin around. A hideous creature that looks like a black hound with bat's wings bounds down from the rocks. You just have time to notice a red chain around its throat before it leaps at you with a wild screech.

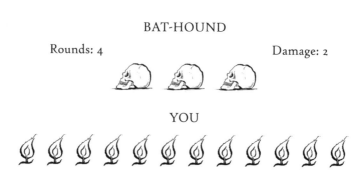

BAT-HOUND

Rounds: 4   Damage: 2

YOU

If you win, turn to **406**.

If you lose, turn to **433**.

76

Before Joe can react, you rush across to the ladder and pull it away. It lands on his workbench with a loud clatter and sends tools and wood shavings flying in all directions.

"Sorry, Joe," you say quietly. "I've spoiled your work."

"What are you doing?" he asks. "They'll catch you like they caught me."

You turn for the door.

"They haven't yet."

Unfortunately, it won't take Joe long to climb down and alert the city guards, so until you're told otherwise, roll two DICE at the end of every new entry. Roll them **after** completing that entry, but **before** turning to the next one. If you roll a double, make a note of what entry you're on, then turn to **372**.

Now, if you had a SILVER RING, delete it from your LOG BOOK, as it was lost in your struggle with Joe. Then turn to **295**.

77

In the end, you make it as far as the junction, before the shadow stops its games and then your heart. Your quest is over.

78

Seagulls wheel and cry and a cold mist rolls in off the sea and up the streets of Port Darktide. The way down to the docks is quiet and still. You think of Old Joe and how much he'd like to be here with you, telling you tales from his early years as a ship's carpenter on the *Shooting Star*.

"I had to splice our mast with an oar, once," he'd say. "That was a long journey back to port."

He likes to talk about his time at sea, but although his voice sounds the same when he tells his stories, his eyes look sad. He keeps a necklace with an anchor pendant beneath his pillow, and you've never found out why.

You're jolted from your thoughts by loud cries and pounding feet. Someone emerges from the mist, runs past and disappears. Her eyes were wild with fear. You peer down the street but the mist is too thick to see far. What was she running from? You edge further down and come to a point where the street splits in two. The main road carries on round to the left and is lit by weak sunlight. You can just make out the looming masts of great ships in the docks below. On the right, a dark, narrow lane splits off into the mist. From there, a boy's voice calls out with a fierce whisper: "Don't go that way – didn't you hear?"

If your SIXTH SENSE level is 5 or higher, turn to **401**.

If it's 4 or lower, turn to **246**.

79

You run across to Casper and frantically search for a way to release him from the pillar. A look of surprise flits across Creeval's face.

"There is a warrior inside that young body of yours," he says. "Your mother would be proud. But I'm afraid you won't help your friend that way."

He laughs as the sound of running feet approaches. Guards

stream into the cavern and form a circle around you. When he speaks again, a new note has entered his voice. Something has occurred to him.

"You have one chance. Only one. If you discover how to free your friend, he and his crewmates will be released unharmed. I give you my word. But in return, you must stay here with me."

If you accept his offer, turn to **96**.

If you don't, turn to **415**.

80

You dart towards the stables. Grabbing the gate, you pray that its old wooden planks won't give way under your weight. They don't, but did you get over in time? You hear boots on the far side of the street. They stop. Your heart's beating so loudly you're sure they're going to hear. But after a muffled conversation your pursuers take off up the street towards the square. You slump against the wall.

Gain 1 ABILITY point and turn to **410**.

81

You look down the path that leads to the Old Lady. When you turn back, Nettle has disappeared. Taking a deep breath, you set off. The ancient trees are twisted into strange shapes, and somehow you feel them watching as you pass. There's no birdsong, or even a breath of wind to stir the branches. Then a cry up ahead shatters the silence. You round the bend and come across a fork in the path. On the right-hand path, you see the source of the cry. It's Nettle calling and beckoning you to follow her! She's eating an apple from a nearby tree. The ground around her is dappled with sunlight. The left-hand path heads even deeper into the forest. The trees are dark and leafless, and ravens brood silently on their branches.

Look closely at the picture opposite.

If you decide to take the left path, turn to **412**.

If you want to follow Nettle down the right path, turn to **70**.

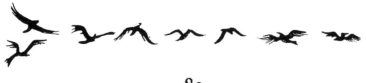

82

Madoc's eyes narrow, but he nods and keeps watch while you hurriedly rummage through the workshop. You have time to stash **either** a ROPE WITH HOOK or a MAGNIFYING GLASS. If you've already picked up one of these items, pick the other one up now. Add the chosen item to your LOG BOOK.

Then, with a final glance back, you set off for his cottage.

Turn to **380**.

83

"That's right, young Rowan," Odan calls.

He grabs your arm to pull you behind the crate, but the grip is too tight and doesn't loosen. You turn around and meet his eyes. They stare back blankly.

"Nobody ever notices, do they? The shadow that's not quite right?"

His shadow capers horribly. It reaches over and touches your foot with a theatrical stretch. The touch is like ice.

"He's just showing off, but he can never quite copy me, even when he's trying," Odan smiles. "Now, this may feel a little cold..."

The shadow's fingers slide up to your temples. You struggle with all your fading strength, but Odan holds you down. A numbness reaches inside your head, and your eyelids flicker shut.

Turn to **241**.

84

She leads you up a steep tunnel that opens onto a broad passageway. Black marble statues line the way. Whether they're gods or monsters is hard to tell. Green flames flicker and cast leaping shadows on the walls.

Turning left takes you back to the junction, so you gesture to the others to follow you the other way.

Turn to **114**.

85

You force yourself to keep your pace slow and measured. It feels like your heart's beating a hundred times between each step, but you're moving quicker than you think. No carts come to a sudden halt and block the way, no traders grab you by the arm and force you to view their dubious merchandise. In fact, you're surprised to see that your turning is coming up.

Suppressing a sigh of relief, you turn off into a side street.

If you have a CITY GUARD'S BADGE, turn to **429**.

If you don't, turn to **275**.

86

If you've given up Flynt, you must subtract 1 from each dice roll. For example, if you roll for 7 or more to do 1 damage, you must roll 8 or more to be successful. But remember, you can still use your armour bonus.

OLD PIRATE

Rounds: 6   Damage: 2

YOU

If you win, turn to **184**.

If you lose, turn to **287**.

87

You fight against people hurrying to market, and progress is slow. Then you spot a side street that leads towards the Craftsmen's Quarter. This forgotten back way was one of the grandest streets in Old Helmsgard, but now its statues are so weathered that you can't tell who or what they once were. A few shops cling on, windows misty with cobwebs, dried herbs hanging over their doorways.

Roll one DICE and add it to your SIXTH SENSE level.

If your total is 7 or higher, turn to **338**.

If it's 6 or lower, turn to **69**.

88

The alchemist's words race through your mind: '*If you ever face anyone that uses a magic staff like me, open this... open this...*'

You take out the pouch and pull the string. A fierce wind fills the chamber. The powder falls through your fingers and swirls like a snowstorm, and in the centre of the storm a shape appears. A bird with great wings slowly flapping. It turns towards your brother with a terrible cry. A bolt from his staff passes harmlessly through its chest and it wrenches the staff from his grasp. Wheeling about, it flies back into the storm, getting smaller and smaller, as if disappearing over the horizon. Then it's gone.

After a moment's silence, your brother turns towards you.

"So, Rowan, any more tricks in that bag of yours?"

"Only one," you reply.

"The fuel," he says with a smile.

Turn to **413**.

89

In the moonlight, everything looks different from how you remember. Old houses lean over the street and rats scuttle down foul-smelling alleyways. You turn into a lane that seems familiar, but the further you go the narrower it gets. It comes out on a cobbled road and you stop dead. The hooded strangers are running straight for you – you're right back where you started! After a fierce but brief struggle they have your face pressed against the cobbles.

"He's too much trouble to take alive," one of them says in a harsh accent.

"You never should have run," another snarls.

They leave your body for the rats to find. The treacherous Tangles have claimed another victim.

90

Rage drives you on. What hope is there? But you won't let this empty shell of a man be the end of you! How many sailors has he betrayed? Fishing routes, nearby vessels, all the information they'd need to intercept a ship at sea. With a roar you didn't even know you possessed, you drive Odan back. He trips and falls, and you stamp down on his cutlass and run him through. His shadow flies from Heston, but too late. Its icy fingers reach straight for your heart, and you lurch to the side to put the mast between you. Heston lies on the floor, clutching his own heart and gasping for breath. The hatch is shut. You're trapped at last.

But then a sinister voice comes from the deck above, speaking a language you don't understand – and the shadow retreats.

You rush over to Heston and he grasps your hand.

"I'll be right enough, Rowan. What's 'ee sayin'?"

The voice is speaking again, but this time in your own language. There's something familiar about it... You creep over to the hatch and inch it open.

Turn to **358**.

91

You turn off and follow the route taken by the guard. It descends steeply even further underground and the walls glisten with ice. Eventually, the tunnel levels out and you find yourself edging along a narrow passage. Up ahead, a green glow lights your way. It's the entrance to a large chamber. You creep forwards and see the guard dragging someone from a cell at the far end. You've found the dungeons. A roar comes from inside the cell.

"Cowards!"

Even though the cell is dark, you'd know that voice anywhere – it's Captain Hamshanks! Chains shake violently, but the remaining guard doesn't stir.

"Patience," he says. "Your turn will come."

If you have a BOW and one ARROW, and would like to use them, turn to **389**.

If you do not, turn to **252**.

92

As you raise the water to your lips, the leaves of the old tree shiver. But where's the wind that stirs them? You feel none. With a stab of panic you leap back, letting the water fall from your hands. Lying on the ground, you look on in horror as tree roots squirm up through the ground. The imp laughs and helps you to your feet.

"At least you listen to your own senses, young one. This is Old Man Tree, and you nearly stole the water he saves for the birds and beasts of the forest."

You tell her you didn't know.

"Because you didn't listen," the imp replies. "And neither did they. Look close."

She points at the knots that sprout like boils from the tree's trunk. In each you see a face, a wooden carving of despair.

"Are they...?"

"Of course they are, sweetie. Now, why don't you tell me what you're doing all alone this deep in the forest?"

Turn to **20**.

93

The guard is grim and strong and the cold has stiffened your joints more than you realised. With one final thrust he forces Flynt from your hand and backs you up against the wall. He opens the door to the cell and pushes you inside.

Turn to **301**.

94

You twist and kick until you feel the point of something sharp pressed against your side.

"Master would prefer to take you alive," a voice says, so close to your face that you can smell the warm breath through the sacking. "But it's only a preference. If you try to escape, I will kill you."

The accent is harsh and unfamiliar. They bundle you onto a cart and someone jumps up beside you. The driver urges the horses forward, and the cart jerks into motion. Lying on the boards, you hit your head every time you go over a pothole. Eventually, the horses slow and a familiar voice calls out in the darkness.

"Halt! Who goes there?"

Your breath catches in your throat. It's Owen, the gatekeeper! His daughter's in your class at school. You're about to call out, when you feel the sharp jab in your side once more, and you remember the warning that went with it.

If you want to try to get Owen's attention, turn to **353**.

If you decide to keep quiet, turn to **409**.

95

You wake in a chair by the fire. A rug has been thrown over you, and the cat is asleep on your lap. Add 3 LIFE points.

"I think you've already met Boska," Madoc smiles. "He comes and goes as he likes."

After a pause he continues.

"The world must look very different to how it did just a few days ago. Something dark is stirring, and you're caught up in it somehow. I wish I could explain, and protect you better – but these are forces beyond my power. Your mother's message was meant for this day and no other. It will lead you into danger, but it's also your only route out... I'm sorry."

You nod slowly and ask if he'll come with you.

"I can take you as far as the entrance to the sewers."

He sees your expression and his eyes twinkle.

"There's a woman down there, an alchemist. I'm sorry she didn't choose a more glamorous location. For years I didn't realise she'd escaped the attack on your mother's hall. I thought I was the only one. How she did it, I don't know. But she's a strange creature. Even back then she rarely ventured above ground. Said the sunlight interfered with her experiments. And there were many who thought those experiments unnatural. I told her so myself, once, and that's why I can't go with you now. She... holds grudges. But your mother often consulted with her. She may know something about the Flame."

Madoc gets up and draws back the curtains. You're surprised to see red sky above the rooftops – you must have been unconscious for some time.

Turn to **402**.

96

"No!" Casper whispers. "It's a trick!"

You lean in close and mutter the captain's words in his ear: "Don't give them your life until you can make them pay for it."

Creeval holds up a black book.

"Climb the steps," he calls. "If you accept my offer."

Turn to **366**.

97

Almost against your own will, you enter the dark lane.

"Hello?" you call out. "Who's there?"

A tall boy with brown hair emerges from an alcove.

"Hello, Rowan."

You take a step back.

"How did you..."

Your eyes widen in recognition.

"Casper?"

He nods, and you're about to say more when he holds up his hand.

"Wait. First we get off the streets, then we talk."

Leading you along the damp lane, he takes you down to the docks and onto a large fishing trawler.

Turn to **305**.

98

You catch a glimpse of the boy disappearing down the street and take off after him, but everyone seems to be going in the opposite direction. In frustration you shove someone out of the way and get a punch in the jaw for your troubles. When you look up, the boy has disappeared.

Deduct 1 LIFE point and turn to **344**.

99

With a speed that takes Joe by surprise, you manage to cuff his wrists and twist free of his grasp.

"Sorry, Joe," you say quietly.

"What are you doing?" he asks. "They'll catch you like they caught me."

"They haven't yet."

You slide down the ladder.

Unfortunately, it won't take Joe long to climb down and alert the city guards, so until you're told otherwise, roll two DICE at the end of every new entry. Roll them **after** completing that entry, but **before** turning to the next one. If you roll a double, make a note of what entry you're on, then turn to **372**.

Now, delete the HANDCUFFS from your LOG BOOK, and if you had the SILVER RING, delete that too, as it was lost in your struggle with Joe. Then turn to **295**.

100

You were told that the mapmaker was a man, so you study the male traders closely. There's one who catches your eye. He has rolled up parchments and measuring tools in his bag, and ink-stained fingers. He also has a compass tattoo on his arm. You decide he's the most likely mapmaker of the bunch.

You walk up to the table and whisper his name. He looks up with grey, bright eyes. They seem almost too young for a face that's been lined by age. You tell him who sent you, and he nods.

"Come with me," he says.

As you leave the tavern, one of the guards glances your way, but Madoc steps into his line of sight, and he turns away.

"Where's your bracelet?" Madoc asks. "That was to show me you were in trouble."

As you both hurry away from the Weeping Willow, you tell him how you lost it.

Gain 1 ABILITY point and turn to **355**.

101

A tentacle snakes forward and wraps itself around your body. Slowly, almost lazily, it coils its way up to your neck and starts to squeeze.

"Give me nowww what is miiine."

You claw at the tentacle, but it squeezes tighter and tighter until your limp body is drawn down into the water. You'll never see how the riverbanks suddenly bloom with fruit trees and flowers. Nor how they wither and die as the river is poisoned by the destruction He brings, with his inevitable conquest of Arkendale!

102

"This is an irregular turn of events," Pustula says, wringing his hands. "But I must warn you that I am far from defenceless."

Up close, you see two fangs overhanging his bottom lip, dripping with something green. And although he has no legs, his body is like a snake's coil, attached to Gucifer's tongue. Before you have time to think about your next move, he springs towards you.

If you have the BLUE STONE, turn to **6**.

If not, turn to **368**.

103

Your hands shake slightly as you lift the cup to your lips. But the water is cool and fresh, and tastes somehow of spring. You drink deeply, and feel new life flowing through your body.

Gain 1 ABILITY point and 2 LIFE points, then turn to **237**.

104

A desperate scream hangs in the air as the shadow fades. You shiver, and hurry on towards the entrance to the sewers.

Turn to **60**.

105

A ripple rolls through the entire hollow. Instinctively, you cling to the hand as the ground falls away. A pit appears beneath your feet, smelling of rotting flesh and death. The figure was a lure! You've stumbled into the mouth of some monstrous burrowing creature that feasts on passing travellers. And your grip is slipping... you have only moments to act.

If you have FIRECRACKERS and want to use them,
turn to **346**.

If you have a ROPE WITH HOOK and would like to use it,
turn to **27**.

If you have a SLEEPING POTION and decide to use it,
turn to **432**.

If you have none of these, or don't want to use them,
turn to **381**.

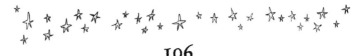

106

The old man leads you back through the bar and into a side room
with a long table and a fire burning in the grate.

"Now then!" he says, rubbing his hands as bread and cheese and
a steaming jug of something spicy are brought through. "Now we
tuck in, and after that, you'll do me the honour of watching a little
theatrical show I'm currently touring."

After you've finished he wipes his mouth and stands up. His
parted lips reveal two long, yellow front teeth. Suddenly his fur
collar starts to twitch and before your eyes it separates into a line of
rats that scuttle along his outstretched arms.

"Steady now, my beauties. 1...2...3!"

The rats stand on their hind legs, join paws and dance a jig while
the old man hums a creaky dirge.

"Bilge rats!" he cries exultantly, as they take a bow. "The best in
the business! Well done my beauties, well done! Cheese to put a
gloss on your fur!" He piles the remaining cheese onto his plate and
they flow down his arm.

"So, child. I trust you've seen nothing to match that in your whole short life?"

You shake your head.

"Just so! Now, I know you haven't much money..." Here his voice takes on a wheedling, sinister quality. "... But I'd take any of the trifles you're carrying as payment."

If you'd like to pay the old man for his show, choose any one item, other than the FUEL or FLYNT, and cross it from your LOG BOOK. Then turn to **240**.

If you decide not to pay him, turn to **427**.

107

In silence, the four figures step forward as one. You're bound and gagged, and a sack is pulled over your head. Then you are carried away like a sack of grain. If you had a HATCHET, delete it from your LOG BOOK.

Turn to **94**.

108

You come to a crossroads. If you want to go:

North, turn to **320**.   South, turn to **57**.

East, turn to **248**.   West, turn to **397**.

109

"Those are not my orders."

It was a long shot. You open your mouth to ask another question, but he tells you to shut it.

Turn to **12**.

In silence, the alchemist runs a finger over the name on the locket. Idriel. Then she mutters something in a language you don't understand and there's a grinding sound as part of the chamber wall slides away to reveal a hidden passage.

She leads you down a flight of spiral steps. Her cane strikes loudly against the stone, and you keep checking behind for the monster. She cackles.

"No need to worry, child. My baby was in no danger – I only showed her to you in a dream. Remember when you first felt dizzy?"

She stops and waggles a long, thin finger in your face.

"I put you to sleep in that first chamber – and you'd still be lying there, as good as dead, if you hadn't surprised me by passing my little test. Why do you think your compass was no help, eh? Nothing makes sense in your dreams!"

She scratches her chin.

"The chalk was a good idea though... Your mind making mental notes... I must rewrite the spell."

Hesitantly, you ask if the monster could have hurt you.

"What's that? Speak up, child."

You repeat the question and she pokes you in the chest.

"I told you once. She's as real as you or me, but you only saw her in your dream. She was born in my lab to fight the coming dark – not a mite like you."

You glance down at your legs and she cackles.

"Those rat bites were real enough, though. This is a sewer, not a palace."

She continues her descent and you follow in silence. It's only when you reach the bottom that you realise you've left your LANTERN, COMPASS and CHALK in the chamber.

Delete them from your LOG BOOK, then turn to **134**.

III

You watch your captor closely and ponder your next move.

If you want to ask him what happened to whole-Harlan, turn to **233**.

If you want to beg him to let you go, turn to **109**.

If you want to ask him why you've been kidnapped, turn to **342**.

If you want to carry on in silence, turn to **12**.

II2

As you take aim, the goblin squeals and makes a run for the long grass.

If you want to stop him escaping, turn to **327**.

If you decide to let him go, turn to **61**.

113

Moving as quickly as you dare through the quiet, orderly streets, you notice a sharp smell hanging in the air. Something like smoke and burnt oil. The further you go the stronger it gets, and when the road tilts downhill you see a group of buildings by the River Wendle that you've never seen before. Timber is being unloaded from barges, and black smoke and red flame rise from great chimneys.

As you approach you hear the roar of giant furnaces and the clang of anvils. The road takes you past the gates, and the sign outside shows a pair of arrows crossed over a shield. Suddenly, the gates open and a cart emerges, loaded with crates. You eye the driver as he flicks the reins. The street is empty, and some extra equipment might come in useful...

If you'd like to jump onto the back of the cart, turn to **238**.

If you'd prefer to continue on your way, turn to **187**.

114

The passageway ends with a set of silver double doors. They're cast with the figure of a man who's separated from his shadow every time you pull them apart. Beyond is darkness. Your footsteps echo as you pass through the entrance. The room must be vast. Suddenly you hear a sound like giant cogs turning, and three rings, one inside the other, start to glow and rotate on the ground in front of you. They're filled with strange markings. Then, with a final clank, everything stops. The markings pulse twice and fade, and a ray of light pierces the blackness. From the roof of a vast cavern it strikes a boy strapped to a pillar in the centre of the rings. He looks up and your eyes meet. It's Casper.

You hear a laugh from the far side of the room. It's a cold, sickly laugh that you've heard too many times already. There he stands, tall and pale, at the top of a flight of steps carved into the rock.

"Welcome, Rowan. What a pleasant surprise! If I'd known you were going to deliver yourself straight into my hands, I'd not have travelled all the way to Helmsgard to knock on your door."

Out of the corner of your eye, you see three guards approaching.

"Dead or alive, Lord Creeval?" one of them calls.

"Alive."

If you have freed the rest of the crew, turn to **308**.

If you haven't, turn to **286**.

115

"His name was Althor. He was, I think, your mother's only true friend. I don't know how they met, because he was from Helmsgard and she was not. He knew Old Joe, and said he could be trusted. Whoever raised you could never know who you were. It was the safest way."

"Idriel and Althor," you say quietly.

He nods, and you ask to see the parchment.

Turn to **259**.

You return bent-backed and sweating, carrying a crate filled with dark brown bottles. You set it down with a loud clink on the stone quay. Captain Hamshanks bursts out laughing.

"Make yerselves known, you dogs!" she roars, and the crew all shout their names. Take a good look at them, and make a note of anything particularly unusual you spot, then turn to **266**.

117

In the half-dark you scatter the caltrops and back away.

Roll one DICE and delete the CALTROPS from your LOG BOOK.

If you roll 1-4, turn to **328**.

If you roll 5-6, turn to **205**.

118

You stare and stare and run your hands over every inch of the great stone doors, but you can see no way to open them.

Deduct 1 ABILITY point.

If you want to bang on the doors to get someone's attention, turn to **430**.

If you want to return to Heston, turn to **218**.

119

"So, it's done," she says. "Look at me."

She pinches your chin between her long fingers and stares into your eyes.

"The fate of Arkendale is held in here."

She hands you a small, leather drinking flask. Carefully, you ease out the stopper. The liquid looks dark in the dim light, but then you notice something else. The low murmur of many voices, and above them a lone, clear voice, singing in a language you don't understand. You push the stopper back in, and the song stops.

Add the FUEL to your LOG BOOK.

"Good. I've done what I can... But now I'm at a loss, Rowan. Where is the Flame? Where is it? The fuel is worthless without the location – and that's a secret passed down from Guardian to Guardian. You were so young..."

She looks at you with a desperate kind of hope. Your eyes widen and you scrabble around in your bag for the book of fairy tales. You turn to the picture and tell her what Madoc said about a flame beneath an oak, in a place that no longer exists. The alchemist stares thoughtfully at the page.

"In a place that no longer exists... I wonder..."

She snaps the book shut and hands it back. Then she puts her fingers to her lips and whistles loudly.

Turn to **263**.

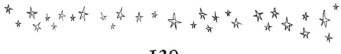

120

As the shadow blade drops from your frozen grasp, you see the guard nod with satisfaction. One of his superiors will take the blade to the Dark Tower, as proof of the Shadow Reaper's final victory.

121

Coughing and spluttering, your throat choked with soil, you clamber clear of your open grave. Laughter floats through the forest, but this time with a note of warmth. The trees part to reveal a wide clearing, bathed in sunlight. You see a hunched figure wrapped in a shawl, drawing up water from a well.

Turn to **386**.

You run down, and as you help Casper to the ground, Creeval speaks in a soft voice that somehow fills the cavern.

"My guards will escort your friend and his crew to the surface. And you, Casper: I advise you to use your brain. You cannot help. The sun is already low in the sky. If I do not see you offshore by the time it sets, Rowan will suffer the fate that was reserved for you. All of you will."

Suddenly you're both surrounded by guards. Before he's led away, Casper leans over.

"Find a way," he says, with a fierce, choked whisper. "Like we always did."

Turn to **160**.

123

You dig the firecrackers from your bag and hurl them at the goblins. The first blast slows them down, the second brings them to a halt, the third sends them running for cover. One of the goblins realises his loincloth is on fire, and jumps into a stagnant pool to put it out. He chatters angrily, waist-deep in slime, and all the marsh goblins join in, yelping and shaking their spears from the safety of the long grass. But when you turn to go, they do not follow.

Delete the FIRECRACKERS from your LOG BOOK,
then turn to **157**.

124

You parry blows that send a dull ache shooting up your arms. But desperation makes you quick. Diving under his heavy mace, you roll and strike. His back arches and he grunts in surprise. Slowly, unbelievably, he falls like a felled oak. You wipe Flynt clean on his tunic. Gain 1 ABILITY point.

Looking around, you remember where you are. You'll have to get out of the square before more guards arrive. But where's the man you're supposed to find? All the traders have disappeared. All except one. He shuffles past with a bag slung over his shoulder. You stop him and ask for Madoc.

Turn to **242**.

125

Gain 1 ABILITY point.

You drop down and pull the hatch shut. A single oil lamp lights the gloomy hold and you stoop to avoid hitting your head on a beam. As you straighten up, you hear a sharp whisper.

"Over here! Rowan!"

In the darkest corner, old Heston Gurgle is crouched behind a pile of nets. You're about to rush over when the hatch is thrown open and Odan Britches sticks his head down. He sees you and smiles.

"There you are!"

His head disappears, then his baggy red britches appear through the hatch. He drops down and his shadow follows, spreading out behind him like a dark cloud.

"So, you don't trust me, Rowan? Was it my shadow? He never gets me quite right, even when he's trying. But I've been here so long they don't notice. They don't even look!"

His words sound triumphant, but his voice is level and his eyes are blank.

"But then you come on board and I see your suspicious glance, so I send out the signal. 'Best this ship doesn't return to port,' I think to myself."

His voice rises for the first time, and his shadow capers and dances horribly.

"You should have said something when you had the chance, Rowan..."

Then he stops abruptly.

"Maybe he still will," a wheezy voice hisses by his ear.

Heston has crept up and pressed his cutlass against his side. But Odan's shadow shifts, and he cries out in pain as it reaches for his heart. You draw Flynt and charge.

Rounds: 5   Damage: 2

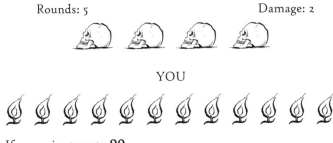

YOU

If you win, turn to **90**.

If you lose, turn to **324**.

126

With one final look around the chamber, you make your way back to the junction.

Turn to **165**.

127

"What old friend?" you shout down in a brave voice. "It's a strange time to come knocking."

You glance around the room to assess your options. Your work belt hangs on the wall, and a hatchet hangs from the belt.

"You have so much to learn, little foundling!" the man calls. "Left on a carpenter's doorstep – maybe on a night such as this!"

He laughs.

"Have you ever wondered who you really are, Rowan?"

Suddenly you hear footsteps around the side of the house. You don't have a moment to lose.

If you want to open the door and talk to the stranger,

turn to **276**.

If you want to fasten the belt over your tunic and escape into the alley behind the workshop, turn to **185** and add a HATCHET to your LOG BOOK.

128

The man you remember sitting with his feet propped up by the fire, smoking his pipe with Old Joe, the man who used to tell you tall tales thought up during his long hours on watch, that good man now watches impassively as your blood trickles between the cobbles. Your quest is over.

129

The three guards rush towards you. You'll have to fight them all at once.

If you lose a round, add together the damage ratings of all three guards (not forgetting to deduct your armour bonus from them all first), then take the total from your LIFE points. If a guard is dead, don't add their damage rating. If you win a round, deduct the COMBAT points only from the guard you chose to attack. Remember to keep a note of how many rounds you have left for each guard.

FIRST GUARD

Rounds: 4 Damage: 3

SECOND GUARD

Rounds: 2 Damage: 2

THIRD GUARD

Rounds: 3 Damage: 2

YOU

If you win, turn to **79**.

If you lose, turn to **272**.

130

You tread on something soft. There's a fierce, spitting yowl and a huge tomcat sinks his teeth into your leg. You spin around and the room keeps spinning. You fall and hit your head against the wall. The room goes black.

Deduct 1 LIFE point and turn to **95**.

131

You feel a sharp pain on your ankle – you've been bitten by a rat. Deduct 1 LIFE point. Then you come to a crossroads. If you want to go:

North, turn to **306**. South, turn to **57**.

East, turn to **320**. West, turn to **204**.

132

Your senses are overpowered by Gucifer's breath and Pustula's venom. Sweat pours down your face and stings your eyes. You take a wild swing and stagger back a fatal step too far... Gucifer swallows. Your quest ends in the sea demon's stomach.

133

You land and roll onto a patch of ice that slips you neatly into the water. Your hand brushes something hard and you instinctively grasp hold. It's this that saves you from going under. With the last of your strength you haul yourself up a rusting ladder and onto the dock. Somehow, you've made it down in one piece.

Deduct 2 LIFE points, then turn to **220**.

The staircase leads down to a wide chamber. Here, the alchemist turns.

"So, they're making their move, are they? Idriel said you would come."

She looks you up and down with a critical eye.

"Younger than I was hoping, and shorter. Who sent you?"

She scowls and spits on the floor when you tell her.

"That jumped-up scarecrow's still alive, is he?" she mutters, shuffling about the room.

You're in a laboratory filled with potions of many colours. Above your head, bats hang from the rafters and ravens perch.

"Ah, there it is!"

The alchemist uses her cane to dislodge a heavy book from a shelf. It hits the floor and sends up a thick cloud of dust.

"Put it on the table," she orders.

Grabbing a magnifying glass, she leafs through the book's yellowed pages. When she looks up, she forgets to put the glass down, and her left eye appears twice the size of her right.

"585th Guardian of the Flame, bud of those ancient roots and Steward of Arkendale, welcome to your servant's wretched quarters."

She bows ceremoniously, and shows you the long list of names, with yours at the bottom and your mother's above. After a moment's silence, she snaps back to her old self.

"Now stop staring and start listening," she says, rapping you on the head with her cane.

"The trouble is you took your world for granted. You didn't imagine there could be any other way. But there are many. The

Guardians are the only reason you haven't seen them. It's their Flame that keeps the darkness at bay. A good harvest, clean water, protection from plague, pestilence, black magic – all this can disappear from Arkendale as easily as a candle is snuffed out by the wind. And what then?"

You open your mouth but she bangs her cane on the ground.

"Then He will come."

If you want to ask who 'He' is, turn to **181**.

If you want to ask what the Guardian does, turn to **234**.

135

You scrabble for traction but the cobbles are greasy and the tailgate slips from your grasp. You're left face-down in the road as the cart trundles up the hill. You lift your head to see a couple of guards rounding the bend. The chance has gone. You climb to your feet and head for the old docks further downriver.

Turn to **187**.

136

When you wake, the sun is already well past midday. You hurry downstairs and thank the innkeeper before you leave.

"Ask Joe to come by when he returns," he says.

You hear the concern in his voice that he tries to hide.

"And take this. Just in case."

He hands you a weapon with a name carved into its hilt: 'Flynt'.

"The serving boy found it this morning, two streets from here. Whoever dropped it was going too fast to notice. You got here just in time, Rowan."

Add FLYNT to your LOG BOOK, then turn to **435**.

137

Your opponent ducks under your flailing attack and tackles you to the ground. He grabs your hand and smashes it against a rock until Flynt drops from your grasp. Dazed and bleeding, you look up to see the deathly white leader striding over. His sightless eyes stare down at you and his thin mouth twists into a smile.

"You are your mother's child, Rowan. But you've caused enough trouble for today. It's time to sleep now."

He raises his hand, and even though you fight it with all your strength, you feel your eyelids closing.

Turn to **241**.

138

"Madoc!" the trader shouts. "There's a kid here wants to meet you!"

A man with grey hair looks up, and his eyes widen in recognition. This, finally, must be the man you've been searching for. But his expression changes to alarm as one of the city guards leaps to his feet.

"That's the one!" he cries. "You're coming with us!"

Roll one DICE and add it to your SKILL level.

If your total is 7 or higher, turn to **251**.

If it's 6 or lower, turn to **369**.

139

The final beast falls from the sky with a screech that's lost to the wind. Wowl's fur glistens with sweat, but his wings beat steadily and his golden eyes roll back briefly to meet yours.

"We made it!" you yell, punching the air.

A roar rips from your throat as fields, forests and villages rush beneath you until they're almost a blur. Helmsgard is left far behind, and as the sun sets, a thin line glitters on the horizon – Port Darktide approaches, and the sea beyond.

Turn to **156**.

140

The hooded figure gives a harsh cry as you burst through the gateway on the back of the horse. With a tug on the reins you veer towards The Tangles. Sparks fly off your steed's hooves as you urge her on. Looking over your shoulder you see that the hooded figure hasn't moved. The others join him on the brow of the hill, and he points in your direction. As the dark streets of The Tangles close around you, the horse gallops on as you leap from the saddle.

Turn to **194**.

141

You dodge behind barrels and boxes, but the shadow just slides over them and keeps on coming. Its every touch drains the life from your body, and eventually it backs you up against the stern of the ship. Slowly, its arms flow up your sides. It feels like ice creeping through your veins.

All around, you see your crewmates fighting a desperate retreat. Cork-eared Karl throws himself furiously into the wraiths, flailing left and right for longer than you thought possible. His heart must be frozen inside his chest, but still he swings. Until finally he falls, hitting the deck like the toppling of a great statue.

You sink to your knees.

If you have picked up a SILVER RING, turn to **363**.

If you haven't, turn to **425**.

142

You bring Flynt down hard and the creature screams. Suddenly the walls start to spin, and you feel that same dizziness you felt when you approached the first chamber. In fact, you are in the first chamber. And why are you on the floor? The creature has gone and in its place stands a frail old woman with wild white hair, leaning on a cane.

"Strike my baby, would you?" she asks, in a dry, cracked voice.

She shakes her head and mutters: "What would you understand of my work, worthless child? Go back to sleep and leave me alone."

You wake again to find the chamber empty. The tunnel back to the old docks has disappeared, and in front of you are four passages. One goes north, one goes south, one goes east and one goes west. But it doesn't matter which one you pick, because you're trapped in a never-ending nightmare, created by the alchemist to protect her lair!

143

The startled hog gives an indignant squeal. Slipping through the passage and into the broad street beyond, you're rewarded by the sound of curses in the yard. Your pursuers had not bargained on an angry hog intent on revenge! This gives you precious moments to assess your options.

The street runs uphill towards the market square, and the city guards have a small station on the other side. During the day, the square is filled with traders, but now it sits empty in the moonlight. You'd be easily spotted in that direction, so it would be a straight race.

Across the street is the entrance to a stables. It's a good place to hide, although you'd be cornered if they found you, and you must climb over a wooden gate to get in.

Your final option is to head down the street into an area of Helmsgard known as 'The Tangles'. People have warned you of this district, full of misfits and thieves, but its maze of crooked passages may just aid your escape.

If you decide to make a run for the city guards at the station, turn to **196**.

If you choose to hide in the stables, turn to **80**.

If you opt for The Tangles, turn to **293**.

144

Gripping the shadow blade, you advance to meet your brother. As he keeps flickering between his body and his shadow, you can't be sure whether your weapon will hurt him. So after every successful attack, roll one DICE.

If you roll a 4-6, your strike was successful and you can deduct his COMBAT points as normal. But if you roll a 1-3, your blade passes right through his body and you cannot deduct any COMBAT points.

Rounds: 8   Damage: 4

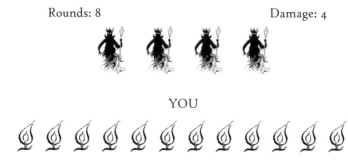

YOU

Leather armour doesn't work against the Shadow Reaper. You can only use a defence bonus if you have a CHAINMAIL VEST. Also, if he still has his staff, whenever you roll a double you're hit by a purple bolt, and must deduct 1 LIFE point regardless of whether you win or lose the round.

If you win, turn to **297**.

If you lose, turn to **391**.

145

You search everywhere, but find no sign of the numbers marked on the parchment. The wind has died down and the tree's reflection lies still on the water. You pick up a pebble and shatter the image.

Slowly it pulls itself back together and the lines from the parchment ripple through your mind. 'You just need time for a little reflection...'

Your eyes widen. It's there, in the water. You can't see it in the tree because it's upside down. A number! 45. You unroll the parchment and see that 45 marks NE on the compass. That leads you back to the third line: 'From numbers to letters to numbers once more.' Perhaps NE are the letters? And then you see the code in the margin: A=1, B=2, C=3... With your heart beating fast, you work out that N=14 and E=5. 145.

You scramble around to the point of the lake that lines up with 145 on the parchment. 'The lake is entered from only one place...' The water is dark and still like a mirror. You close your eyes and take a step forwards.

Your foot lands on something hard and cold. You open your eyes and find yourself standing on a flight of steps leading down into the lake. How did you not see it before? Was it even there? You touch the top step and your hand comes away wet, yet it feels like stone beneath your feet.

You walk down into darkness.

Gain 1 ABILITY point, then turn to **294**.

146

With a speed that takes Joe by surprise, you cuff his free wrist to the wooden railings by your bed. He built them to stop you from rolling off the platform when you were a baby, and he built them well. They'll hold him long enough to make your escape.

You twist free of his grasp.

"Sorry, Joe," you say quietly.

"What are you doing?" he asks. "They'll catch you like they caught me."

"They haven't yet."

You slide down the ladder.

Delete the HANDCUFFS from your LOG BOOK, and if you had a SILVER RING, delete that too, as it was lost in your struggle with Joe. Then turn to **295**.

147

The guard somersaults over you and whips the chain around your neck. You fall to your knees, gasping for breath. As the torchlight fades, she bends down and peers into your eyes. It's the last face you ever see.

148

Have you picked up the BOOK OF FAIRY TALES from the workshop?

If you have, turn to **321**.

If you haven't, turn to **39**.

149

Knowing you don't have a moment to lose, you lever the lid from the crate. It lifts without a sound. Peering inside, you see chainmail vests gleaming with a strange, dark sheen.

If you don't already have a CHAINMAIL VEST, add it to your LOG BOOK and delete the LEATHER ARMOUR. The vest gives some protection against shadow wraiths, so make a note that it decreases **any** opponent's DAMAGE RATING by 1 LIFE point.

Turn to **10**.

150

You tell her that's your business and yours alone. Her green eyes narrow. Then she breaks into a gold-toothed grin.

"I like this one!" she says to Casper.

Turn to **161**.

151

With your free hand you work the flower loose. Its petals are so thin and dry that you're worried it will fall apart in your trembling hands. You hold it out – a small white star in the gloom of the old docks. A dark hand stretches to meet it, and something strange happens. The petals of the flower start to darken and fade, until they're nothing but shadow themselves. A sound halfway between a sigh and a sob drifts through the damp air, then all is still.

Cautiously, you stretch out a hand. The shadow is no longer cold, no longer moves. It's turned into a monument made of shadow. A monument to whole-Harlan. You've fulfilled your promise.

You turn and head towards the entrance to the sewers.

Gain 3 ABILITY points, delete the WHITE FLOWER from your LOG BOOK, then turn to **60**.

152

The shadow drifts apart with a lonely cry and you dart into a street on the opposite side of the square.

If you have a CITY GUARD'S BADGE, turn to **429**.

If you don't, turn to **275**.

153

You send his fancy hammers spinning across the ground, and hold Flynt to his throat.

"Wait!" Woad snivels. "I heard my father talking – that's why I followed. I saw you on the high street. They're looking for you, Rowan." He pauses, breathing deeply. "You're heading for your workshop, aren't you? You're wasting your time. They sent Joe a letter saying his brother was ill." A snigger escapes his lips. "It's a two-day journey just to find out he's been tricked!"

You stare at him in confusion, and he rolls from under your foot. Before you can react, he's off and running down the street. Instinctively, you pick up one of his hammers.

If you want to throw it at the retreating Woad, roll one DICE and add it to your SKILL level.

If your total is 8 or higher, turn to **244**.

If it's 7 or lower, turn to **170**.

If you don't want to throw the war hammer, turn to **195**.

154

Your hand goes to your belt, and with an ease born of countless days in the workshop, you slide the hatchet loose. This small axe was only meant for trimming wood, but it's better than no weapon at all. The hooded figure steps forwards, and you think back to your basic combat training with the other children of the neighbourhood. They never said anything about fighting with a hatchet! You shift it from hand to hand in what you hope is an intimidating gesture, but the effect is ruined when you drop it on the floor. As you scrabble to pick it up, the man draws his own weapon and waits.

Because you only have the HATCHET, you must subtract 1 from each dice roll. For example, if you roll for 7 or more to do 1 damage, you must roll 8 or more to be successful.

HOODED FIGURE

Rounds: 5   Damage: 2

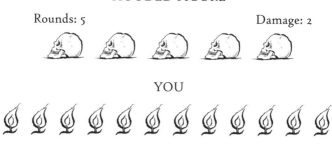

YOU

If you win, turn to **349**.

If you lose, turn to **53**.

155

The clouds darken and the water ripples, stirred by an unseen force.

"Child, if you couldn't overcome my simple test, you would be no help to me. Far greater challenges lie ahead."

The water threatens to overspill the bucket, and you take a step back. The trees close in and loom over you. They await their orders. Then the sound of laughter rolls around the clearing and the trees retreat.

"But you are right to be suspicious, and it took courage to ask.

Perhaps there is hope after all. So, drink this – a gift from the forest."

The figure scoops water from the bucket with a wooden cup and holds it out.

If you want to drink the water, turn to **103**.

If you would prefer just to set off back for Helmsgard,

turn to **237**.

156

The moon marks a pale path across the sea. You left Port Darktide behind many hours ago, and torchlight from the odd merchant ship passes in the blink of an eye. You lie pressed against Wowl's warm fur, drifting in and out of sleep. Add 5 LIFE points.

Suddenly you feel a soft growl and raise your head. There it is – the Lonely Isle, silhouetted against the moon. As it grows larger you see it's little more than a rocky outcrop for nesting birds. Wowl lands at the top of a cliff-face, his great paws skittering on rocks worn smooth by the wind and rain. You climb down and he takes off once more. Three times he circles the island, before turning for the mainland with a howl. You're left alone.

A short scramble sends loose stones bounding over the cliff edge, and finally you're up over the crest. In front of you is a small, black lake. On the other side is the tree – just like it showed in your storybook. You skirt the lake and reach the tree. There's no symbol on its trunk, and no sign of a hidden entrance. You continue around back to where you started and take out the alchemist's parchment.

Turn the page to see the parchment, the tree and the lake. If you follow the clues correctly you'll find the entrance.

A=1 B=2

The lake is entered from only one place,
Use the compass or suffer an icy embrace.
From numbers to letters to numbers once more,
But where's the first number? Not on the shore.
All becomes clear on closer inspection,
You just need time for a little reflection.

C=3 D=4

When you think you've found the final numbers, put them together and turn to that entry. If you can't find the right numbers, turn to **58**.

157

You continue your journey towards Port Darktide. It must still be the early hours of the morning, and the sentries at the gate eye you suspiciously.

"Helmsgard?" one of them says with a thick western accent. "That's a week's hard riding. How've you come all that way?"

You tell them you're visiting a friend and had meant to arrive before dark.

"A friend, you say. Who's that then?"

"Casper."

It's a boy you know who moved to Darktide a few years ago.

"You know anyone by that name, Gus?"

The other guard rubs his chin.

"Fishing family?" he asks.

You nod.

"I knew his father," he says, with a slight grimace.

The first guard is quiet for a moment, then says more softly:

"Alright, kid. You can pass. Just keep to the main streets, if you know what's good for you."

They step aside and you walk through the gateway and into Port Darktide.

If you'd like to head straight for the docks, turn to **78**.

If you'd prefer to rest first and get something to eat, turn to **279**.

158

No torches burn here, but a faint blue light filters through from the sky far above. After many twists and turns, it leads you to a stone chamber. On the back wall there's a small iron hatch.

If you'd like to open the hatch, turn to **284**.

If you'd like to go back and take the other turning, go to **354**.

159

The hooded stranger fights in silence and his expression never changes – even when you strike the final blow. He falls to the floor as Madoc runs through the doorway.

"We've been lucky," he says grimly. "I did not expect them to send six men to ambush one child. You must have their respect, Rowan."

He looks around the workshop.

"We should hurry. The night is quiet and we were loud – reinforcements could be on their way."

Turn to **193**.

160

Creeval mutters something in a low voice, and a door appears in the wall behind him.

"Come, Rowan."

You follow through the doorway and gasp. You're standing in a room at the top of a tall tower. On three sides you're surrounded by the white flanks of great peaks, and the grey sea stretches away to the south.

"You're a long way from home, carpenter's child."

He smiles a sickly smile and pinches your chin so that you're forced to stare into his white eyes. His breath stinks of decay.

"You know where it is, don't you? The Flame. That's where you were sailing for."

He lets go.

"I said I would release your friends if you completed a task, and you saw how I kept my word. You have the heart and mind of a Guardian. She would have entrusted the secret to you, somehow. Your mother."

He looks past you and out to sea.

"So, I make you another... offer. If you lead me to the Flame, I will spare you."

You make no reply as the wind whistles around the tower. Your eyes take in a room filled with books and strange artefacts. In the centre, green flames flicker in an iron hearth. A table with a chessboard stands to one side.

Creeval continues.

"But perhaps before you answer, you should learn your current fate. You have seen the Dial. You know that it cuts your body from your shadow. But do you know what that really means?"

"That you die, but your shadow lives." Turn to **407**.

"That you live, but your shadow dies." Turn to **232**.

"That you both live, but split apart." Turn to **336**.

161

"Alright, dearie, we'll take you. It'll cost you one item from your satchel. We'll negotiate the price for your passage back once you're there!"

She turns and winks at her crew, who are readying the ship to set sail. They roar with laughter. You don't like it, but you think of a flame guttering and swallow your pride. Every hour is precious. Choose any item except for the FUEL or FLYNT and delete it from your LOG BOOK.

The captain inspects it closely, then leans down and produces a dirty piece of paper from inside her boot.

"Pick up these supplies from the warehouse at the end of the dock. Then I'll introduce you to the crew."

Turn to **116**.

162

Through blue lips, you gasp an apology for trying to drink the water. But the imp shakes her head and the roots tighten ominously.

"It's not about the water anymore," she sighs.

As your head starts to spin, images flash through your mind of Old Joe teaching you manners as a child. That's it...

"Without asking!" you gasp. "Without asking!"

The roots uncoil and you fall to the ground.

"That's better, sweetie," the imp chuckles as she helps you up.

"He saves that water for the birds and beasts of the forest. Not outsiders who don't ask nicely. Come to mention it, what are you doing all alone this deep in the forest?"

Deduct 1 LIFE point and turn to **20**.

163

If this is your first incorrect answer, turn to **422**.

If this is your second incorrect answer, turn to **398**.

164

"It's a gunger!" shouts Heston Gurgle, as you haul the ugliest fish you've ever seen on board.

"I cort one too!" cries Cork-eared Karl.

"And me!" says Hairy Jonas.

"So what do we do?" Captain Hamshanks roars from the helm, and Heston roars back: "WE 'AS US A GUNGE FIGHT!"

As the deck is cleared, Casper explains what's going on.

"Whenever we catch gungers, we have a gunge fight. If you press the yellow spot on their belly, they spit out a glob – only one glob, mind – of something strange. It turns you into a big baby. That's the only way I can describe it. Just for a few minutes, but it's funny to watch. Now listen, there's three of you in this fight..."

He leans over and whispers in your ear.

"... and Karl's the best shot."

He claps you on the shoulder and joins the rest of the crew at the helm. You, Jonas and Karl are left facing each other on deck, a few paces apart, with your gungers by your feet.

You weigh up your options. You can't hit both men, because you only have one shot. So the question is, how do you best avoid getting gunged? The captain puts her horn to her lips, and as she blows you bring your gunger up in one smooth movement. Jonas and Karl are still grabbing for theirs, so you get to shoot first.

If you want to gunge Karl, turn to **245**.

If you want to gunge Jonas, turn to **8**.

If you decide to deliberately miss, turn to **253**.

165

You take the other path at the junction, and are just in time to see a guard disappearing down a side passage.

If you'd like to follow him, turn to **91**.

If you'd prefer to continue along the main passage, turn to **329**.

166

You decide this is the chance you've been waiting for!

Roll one DICE and add it to your ATHLETICISM level.

If your total is 7 or higher, turn to **388**.

If it's 6 or lower, turn to **265**.

167

Madoc hands you the bow and arrows.

"Remember, Rowan, it's you they're after. I'll do my best to hold them off, but if there are too many, you won't have much time."

He walks towards the broken door, drags it back and steps inside. You hear raised voices and a scream. Madoc dives outside and rolls to his feet. Moments later, a city guard slumps through the doorway, dead.

Five men step over him with their weapons drawn and quickly surround Madoc. Three are dressed in hoods, like the strangers who woke you in the night. The other two are city guards. They must be working together!

You breathe out slowly to steady your arm, and let fly. The nearest man looks down in surprise as an arrow emerges from his chest. The others spin around.

"Faster!" Madoc cries, and moves to confront one of the guards.

The other three run towards you. There are ten arrows left in your quiver. You draw one and take aim at the first man...

Roll one DICE. If you roll a...

... 6: you kill him. Fill in both halves of his crossbones below.

... 4 or 5: you wound him. Fill in one half of his crossbones.

... 1, 2 or 3: you miss.

If your SKILL level is 5 or higher, add 1 to each roll. For example, a 3 becomes a 4.

When both halves of his crossbones are filled in, the attacker is dead. After each roll, scribble out one of your ten arrows below.

HOODED FIGURE

CITY GUARD

HOODED FIGURE

If you kill all three attackers before running out of arrows, turn to **72**.

If you run out of arrows before all three have been killed, turn to **14**.

168

There are no trees in the hollow, but it's covered in some kind of thick grass. As you climb down, it feels wet and slightly sticky. The cries for help become more urgent. You hurry across, checking for danger, but see nothing other than the black treetops swaying above the rim of the hollow. There's no breeze down here. In fact, it's quite warm.

The boy's face is difficult to make out, even now you're standing over him. But his hand is outstretched and you reach down. Why's it so clammy and soft? Boneless...

Roll one DICE and add it to your SIXTH SENSE level.

If your total is 9 or higher, turn to **105**.

If it's 8 or lower, turn to **262**.

169

You sink to your knees on the damp path. The shadow reaches out for the white flower, and with the last of your strength, you pluck it from your tunic. As the world around you fades, the shadow holds the flower to the sky, a small bright star in the gathering gloom. Too late, you've fulfilled your promise to half-Harlan.

The hammer spins past Woad's right arm and cartwheels off the cobbles. He picks it up, gives a mocking cry and disappears around the corner.

If you'd like to continue on to the workshop, turn to **344**.

If you'd like to turn back and head for the market, turn to **55**.

If you decide that now is the time to report your attempted kidnapping to the City Guard, turn to **200**.

171

Rowan, I found this parchment hidden between the pages of a book. It shows a secret entrance to the chamber of the Flame. An entrance from the mountain, before the old kingdom flooded. It must be the Lonely Isle – and you can't get in without it. If only I'd known...

But now is not the time for despair. The Flame can be relit, Rowan! Use the diagram to help you find the entrance. Wowl will take you.

And now I go meet my fate. They are in the tunnels and Wowl must stay hidden. They'll not stop until I'm dead. My poor creatures can't hold them off much longer. But you're still alive, I feel it in my bones – and that's why I go with a smile on my lips.

Fly, Idriel's child. Fly!

You look at the diagram on the parchment, but your eyes are streaming in the fierce wind. Carefully, you roll it up with the note and stow them under your tunic. Then you lean down and speak into Wowl's ear.

"To the Lonely Isle. As fast as you can."

Turn to **278**.

172

A spiked metal ball whistles towards you. Diving to one side, you manage to avoid a fatal blow, but blood drips from your fingers. Deduct 1 LIFE point.

A guard dressed all in black steps out from behind a statue. She's whirling the deadly ball above her head. It's on the end of a chain.

"Who approaches the Temple of the Shadow?"

You're about to speak, when she sees your shadow looming on the wall, and attacks.

Turn to **264**.

173

The boy is slippery as a fish. His arms and legs seem to be everywhere at once, and before you realise what's happening, he's got you pinned to the ground, unable to move.

"I don't know why I been attacked," he says, for the benefit of the crowd that's gathered. "I done nothing wrong and don't want no trouble." He looks around. "Maybe I been mistaken for someone else. I don't want nothing that's not mine, I just want to be treated fair."

He releases you and stands up. The crowd murmurs in approval and parts to let him past. With a red face, you dust yourself down. "Shame on you!" someone calls.

Deduct 1 ABILITY point and turn to **344**.

174

You hear shouting coming from down the street, and recognise the voice. It belongs to Woad Griblin, that odious son of Lester Griblin, chief of the guards.

"This way!" he cries. "I saw him heading for the workshop!"

Looking out, you see a group of armed guards running in your direction. Something tells you they're not here to investigate the break-in! You have time to grab your satchel and put **one** item in before making your escape. Choose either: a ROPE WITH HOOK, a HOODED CLOAK or a MAGNIFYING GLASS, and add the item you've chosen to your LOG BOOK.

You stow your chosen item and escape through the back window. There's only one thing on your mind now – to find Madoc at the market. You just hope he's still there.

Turn to **55**.

175

Barrels, nets and other flotsam rain down into the creature's mouth. Gucifer shakes the ship as if it were a child's toy, and you feel the wet mast slipping from your grasp. With a despairing cry, you fall. The black pit of its throat rushes towards you. A yellow tooth flashes past, as big as a man, and you reach out. Your arm is almost jerked from your shoulder and you can't hold on, but the tooth breaks your fall and sends you crashing into the creature's soft tongue. Dazed, dimly aware you have moments left to live, you stagger to your feet. Blood trickles down your hand. Then you see him in the corner of your eye, trying to look inconspicuous, and your head clears – it's Pustula. In an instant, you have Flynt drawn.

"If you swallow," you shout, "I'll take him down with me!"

Deduct 2 LIFE points, then turn to **102**.

176

The symbol slips from your mind as the lure of taking Creeval's mage proves too strong. It's the right move, in terms of the game, but this is a game you're never going to win. Finally, Creeval looks up.

"Have you made your decision, Rowan? Dragon takes Guardian."

You meet his white eyes. You have no choice. And then you see something – a shadow sliding under the window behind his back. He turns, but suddenly they're everywhere; creeping in from all sides, flowing up the walls and across the floor until the table is surrounded. Creeval draws his blade and bares his rotten teeth.

"The Shadow Reaper has made his move. We're too late."

Your quest ends, high in the mountains of the north, side-by-side with the man who started it all.

177

At the bottom of the slope you find yourself wading through tall grass. It reaches up to your chest and the ground is boggy underfoot. You pause to catch your breath. Out of the corner of your eye, you see a ripple moving through the grass, heading in your direction. Then you see another on the other side. Suddenly there are ripples all around, half a dozen of them, making straight for the spot where you stand! Without waiting to find out what's causing them, you run. Six small heads, green and pointy-nosed, spring up from the grass then drop back down. With angry, chattering cries they take off in pursuit.

You make it to the edge of the marshland, but the going is tough and the marsh goblins are gaining. The nearest one is so close that you can see bird skulls hanging from her belt.

If you have CALTROPS and want to use them, turn to **257**.

If you have FIRECRACKERS and want to use them, turn to **123**.

If you have a NET and want to use it, turn to **30**.

If you have none of these items, or don't want to use them, turn to **198**.

178

You daren't look in his direction, and your left eye develops a twitch that you're sure he'll notice.

"Hello, Rowan," he says. "Haven't seen you in a while."

Trying to keep your voice as flat as his, you tell him that you fell ill, but that Old Joe has nursed you back to health.

"That's well," he says. "The Shadow Reaper wishes health and contentment on all his subjects."

"We are truly blessed," you reply, and wonder if you've gone too far.

But Owen nods and moves on.

This is the man who used to teach you rude and inventive ditties about Lester Griblin, his boss. You don't look back, and cover the short distance left to Madoc's as quickly as possible.

Turn to **379**.

179

You ask if the water is poisoned. The leaves above you rustle and the imp chuckles.

"I shouldn't think so, my sweet."

"Then why?"

She cocks her head to one side and points at the tree.

"Because you haven't *asked*."

You turn towards the tree, and the strangest thing happens – its top branches bend down. Almost like it's nodding. You glance around to make sure that no one else is watching, then quietly ask for a drink. A single leaf falls from a branch and lands in the little pool of water.

"That means yes," the imp trills. "Old Man Tree saves that water for the birds and beasts of the forest, but will always be generous to those who ask nicely."

Her voice falls lower.

"Of course, not everyone does ask nicely."

She points at the round knots that sprout like boils from the tree's trunk. In each one you see a face, a wooden carving of despair.

"Now, why don't you tell me what you're doing all alone this deep in the forest?"

You drink a handful of cool, clear water, and begin your story.

Add 2 LIFE points, then turn to **20**.

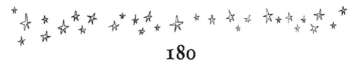

180

You turn away and carry on along the main street. The sunlight is beginning to burn off the mist, and you see shadowy figures working in the docks below. A man is walking up the street towards you.

"Excuse me," he says, in a harsh accent.

Something hard hits you on the back of the head as you're trying to work out where you've heard that accent before. You find yourself lying on the cold cobbles, looking up at two men in dark cloaks. Deduct 1 LIFE point.

"Little more than a child," the first man says. "But old enough to carry a weapon. That's what we were told. Go get the rope."

The second man turns to go, then stops suddenly.

"Get up!" a voice yells. A young voice.

You turn to see a tall boy with brown hair barring the man's way. He's holding a cutlass. You scramble to your feet to face the man standing over you.

Rounds: 6   Damage: 3

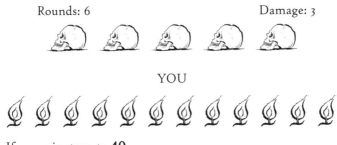

YOU

If you win, turn to **40**.

If you lose, turn to **231**.

181

"I don't know, Rowan. It's the prophecy. But he killed your mother, so he'll make short work of you if he ever catches you. And it's the WRONG QUESTION."

She raps you on the head again, right in the spot that was already tender.

"Don't you want to know what the Guardian does? What He's so scared of? I'll tell you."

Turn to **234**.

182

The cuts from Woad's weapons leave you woozy and weak. Finally, you drop to your knees. As the world goes dark, Woad stands over you and gloats.

"Wait till Father sees what I've found. Maybe I'm not such a useless son after all!"

By the time you come around, you're slung over the shoulder of a huge guard. You see the steps to the guards' station ahead.

"Woad said you'd come round," he grunts.

He puts you down and prods you forward sharply.

"You can save my back and walk up them steps yerself."

Turn to **325**.

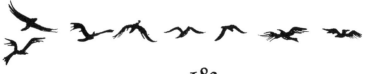

183

You look from the Lonely Isle to the galley, then back to the Lonely Isle.

"Hold course for the island," you say eventually.

You look at Heston, but he says nothing.

"We have to."

He nods towards the galley.

"Aye-aye, Rowan. But we best wait until they're over the horizon, at least."

So you wait, and clear and swab the deck in silence. When they're out of sight, Heston points to one of the ropes.

"Grab that rope, Rowan, and pull when I say."

Together, you hoist the sail.

Turn to **431**.

184

Diving under the notched cutlass you grab the old pirate's peg leg and yank it off. He yells as if you'd amputated his real leg, falls back, and gets tangled up in a hammock. Diabolical curses and threats emerge from the twisted sheeting, until you hit him over the head with his own wooden leg.

As you're leaving, you feel a tap on your shoulder and a voice whispers in your ear.

"You're new to these parts, but you won't last long if you keep drawing attention to yourself like that. Wherever you're going, go there fast, and keep away from the shadows."

You turn around, but whoever it was is already retreating into the dark room.

If you gave up your items and Flynt, you pick them up again now. Then you leave the hostel and head for the docks.

Gain 1 ABILITY point and turn to **78**.

185

You spin around. Earlier in the day, Old Joe was unexpectedly called away. He's the carpenter who's raised you as his own, and without him there's no one to turn to. You pull on your boots and make a bolt for the window at the back of the room. Below is a cobblestoned alley with a clothesline strung across from the house opposite.

Roll one DICE and add it to your ATHLETICISM level.

If your total is 7 or higher, turn to **56**.

If it's 6 or lower, turn to **417**.

186

The force of the arrow catches the guard off balance and knocks him back into the bars. He slumps to the ground.

"Who's there?" calls the Captain.

You step from the shadows.

Delete one ARROW from your LOG BOOK, then turn to **371**.

187

The buildings get older and the air clearer as you near the docks. Taking the deserted path down by the river, you approach the rotten hulk of an old merchant ship. It's leaning towards the shore, sinking year by year into thick mud. The door to the cabin hangs on its hinges and a dark shape slides past the window. You hurry on, hoping it was just a trick of the light, but a shadow flows across the green deck and over the mud.

It comes to a halt on the path in front. You draw your blade.

If you have a WHITE FLOWER, turn to **316**.

If you don't, turn to **192**.

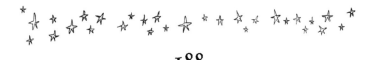

188

The metal ball drops to the stone floor, and the guard slumps down beside it. You drag her body behind a statue before carrying on.

Turn to **114**.

189

You sidestep smartly and leap across the mattress. But you have to steady yourself before leaping to the floor below, and that's what costs you. Joe spins around and makes a grab for your legs. His fingertips hook your ankles in mid-air and send you head-first from the platform. You hold out your arms to cushion your landing and roll as you hit the hard floor. Deduct 3 LIFE points. Dazed and bruised, you stagger to your feet.

Turn to **76**.

And so the game begins. Many times you've played Old Joe on long winter nights after sweeping away the day's sawdust and shavings. But you've never played someone like Creeval. It's soon clear that the game won't last long.

"Do the pieces look familiar?" Creeval asks, as he captures your mage. His white eyes stare.

"I took them from your mother's room."

Your hand shakes as you slide your castle across the board.

"You can keep them, if you accept my offer."

Perhaps it's the mention of your mother, but your thoughts turn to the book of fairy tales, and the message she left for you. Guidance from beyond the grave. Almost mechanically, you move your unicorn, and suddenly the pieces swim in front of your eyes. Then everything snaps back into focus. You sit up in your chair. Your pieces on the board, they remind you of something. It's almost as if someone's been playing through you. Making a shape. A pattern you've seen a lot recently, without even realising it. Images flash in front of your eyes, from the book, the alchemist's laboratory, the dock at Port Darktide...

Turn the page to see the board. Can you work out which square you need to move one of your pieces onto? When you've found the square, count how many in from the left it is, and how many up from the bottom. Put the two numbers together to find its coordinates, and turn to that entry.

If you can't work out the coordinate, turn to **176**.

191

"It is perhaps best not to dwell on the particulars," Pustula replies. "But we have been instructed to service all who approach the isle, in case..."

He clears his throat awkwardly.

"In case they should happen to be frugal with the truth. There is no personal judgement involved, you understand," he adds hastily. "We are not judge and jury."

You find yourself falling in to the creature's peculiar way of speaking.

"I understand completely," you say. "You strike me as most professional in your manner."

Pustula bows.

"But there is one matter on which I am still hazy. Who gave you these instructions?"

Turn to **390**.

192

The shadow surges forwards in that familiar, awful silence.

SHADOW WRAITH

Rounds: 4   Damage: 4

YOU

Leather armour doesn't work against shadow wraiths. You can only use a defence bonus if you have a CHAINMAIL VEST.

If you win, turn to **104**.

If you lose, turn to **261**.

193

The workshop has been ransacked. Tools, materials and broken glass cover the floor. You see with relief there's no sign of Old Joe, but his violin lies smashed and broken in front of the hearth. You pick it up gently. He used to say it was the only thing that got you to sleep when you were a baby, and even now you can hear the sweet, sad music that somehow flows from his rough hands.

Softly, Madoc urges you to look for the book. You climb up to your platform and find your bed overturned. But nothing has been taken. This was a search, not a robbery – and they didn't find it, because they didn't know what they were looking for. You walk over to the corner of the room and pick up a book that was peeking out from under an overturned chest.

"Here it is," you say. "We've got it."

Gain 1 ABILITY point and add a BOOK OF FAIRY TALES to your LOG BOOK.

If you'd like to search for other items that might be useful, turn to **82**.

If you'd like to return to Madoc's cottage straight away, turn to **380**.

194

You dart down an alley and slump behind a barrel to catch your breath. Helmsgard is the city you've always called home, but suddenly you feel very alone. Who are these people? What do they want? Then you remember something that Old Joe said a few weeks ago. You were sweeping up after work and he leant in the doorway with a strange look in his eyes.

"Get to the Cat and Coracle, Rowan. If you're ever in trouble, forget the city guards – get to the Cat and Coracle."

He wasn't a man who wasted words, so you knew that was all you were going to get. But you saw his kindly face trying to mask his concern.

The Cat and Coracle is in The Tangles. You've only been there once before, and that was a long time ago. But at least you entered The Tangles along this same street – that will give you a chance of finding the inn, using your vague memories of the route.

Turn to **47**.

195

It's with a strange mix of relief and annoyance that you watch Woad get away. When he rounds the bend you toss his war hammer aside in distaste.

If you'd like to continue on to the workshop, turn to **344**.

If you'd like to turn back and head for the market, turn to **55**.

If you decide that now is the time to report your attempted kidnapping to the City Guard, turn to **200**.

196

Your breath turns ragged with the effort of keeping ahead of your pursuers. You call for help, but every door and window stays shut. Surely someone must have heard you? Somehow, you make it to the square. If you can just get to the other side, you might be saved!

Roll one DICE and add it to your ENDURANCE level.

If your total is 7 or higher, turn to **330**.

If it's 6 or lower, turn to **373**.

197

You land with a splash in a pool of warm, frothing liquid. Almost at once you feel your skin burning – the creature's stomach juices are starting their work! You cry out in the darkness, but there's no one to hear. In desperation you reach for Flynt and stab downwards. It's like a small fishbone in a creature this large, but it's your only hope.

Deduct 1 LIFE point, then roll one DICE.

If you roll 1-5, deduct 1 LIFE point and roll again.

If you roll 6, turn to **201**.

198

You realise you'll never outrun the goblins, and make your stand on a small mound covered in short grass. They close with their spears raised.

If you snared any in your net, cross them from the list, starting at the bottom.

The goblins give little thought to fighting as a group, so if you lose a round, only count the damage from the goblin you chose to attack. If you win the round, only deduct the COMBAT points from that goblin, too. Remember to keep a note of how many rounds you have left for each goblin.

FIRST MARSH GOBLIN

Rounds: 4   Damage: 2

SECOND MARSH GOBLIN

Rounds: 2   Damage: 2

THIRD MARSH GOBLIN

Rounds: 4   Damage: 2

FOURTH MARSH GOBLIN

Rounds: 2   Damage: 3

FIFTH MARSH GOBLIN

Rounds: 3   Damage: 2

SIXTH MARSH GOBLIN

Rounds: 3   Damage: 3

If you defeat all the goblins, turn to **157**.

If you are defeated by a goblin, turn to **332**.

199

You can't decide which course of action is less risky. You'd still be in the shade if you broke ranks and ran down the middle of the road, but you'd also draw attention to yourself.

If you decide to get to Madoc's as quickly as possible, turn to **367**.

If you'd prefer to stay in line and keep your head down, turn to **85**.

200

The guards' station is on the far side of the market. Using a side road to avoid the crowds, you hear the traders hawking the last of their wares. As you approach the station, you see two guards by the entrance.

If your SIXTH SENSE level is 4 or higher, turn to **11**.

If your SIXTH SENSE level is 3, turn to **325**.

By pure chance, Flynt pricks a nerve. At once, you feel a shudder. And another. Then the whole pit convulses and a great force erupts beneath your feet. You find yourself shooting towards the clear night sky as the contents of the creature's stomach are sent spewing upwards! The partially decomposed head of a bear rides beside you at the crest of the torrent. You're ejected from the creature's mouth with such force that you land back near the path, covered in slime and shaking from your narrow escape.

On the ground next to you, also thick with slime, you see a silver ring carved in the shape of a shield. You shudder and wonder how long it had lain in that foul creature's stomach. After washing both yourself and the ring in a nearby stream, you continue on your way.

Add a SILVER RING to your LOG BOOK, then turn to **157**.

202

"Goodness me, no! The Old Lady doesn't like crowds. You go alone or not at all."

Nettle grips your arm.

"But a word of advice: sometimes the true path is hidden in plain sight. To find the Old Lady, first you have to see her. Yes? Really see her."

If you'd like to set off to find the Old Lady, turn to **81**.

If you'd like to return to Helmsgard, turn to **421**.

203

The guards stand over you, and it's only now you see one of them is Owen the gatekeeper. He's known you since you were a child, and used to bring around a rabbit or two for Old Joe if he'd been out hunting. But now there's not a flicker of emotion on his face. Your adventure ends under his blank gaze, and Woad Griblin has his revenge.

204

You come to a crossroads. If you want to go:

North, turn to **306**.

South, turn to **57**.

East, turn to **9**.

West, turn to **131**.

205

All three guards rush towards you, but two of them cry out and fall to the floor, clutching their feet. Only one guard makes it through your makeshift trap.

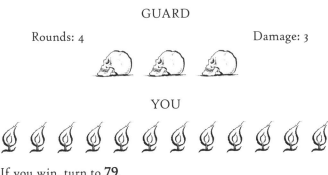

GUARD

Rounds: 4

Damage: 3

YOU

If you win, turn to **79**.

If you lose, turn to **272**.

206

You roll to cushion the impact, and almost end up sliding into the icy waters. But you stop just short and get to your feet. You've jarred your ankle, but it could have been worse.

Deduct 1 LIFE point, then turn to **220**.

207

You walk over to your scorched satchel and fumble inside for the flask. It's intact. Holding it over the basin, you ease out the stopper. In the dim glow from the pit outside, the liquid looks like the night sky. The murmur of many voices fills the chamber, and you hear again the lone, clear voice, singing its ancient song. The fuel bursts into flame the moment it touches the green stone. Suddenly the floor of the chamber is gone. You see roots stretching down into the depths of the earth, and beyond that, stars. Stars all around, shining like the souls of Guardians past. The brightest of them all twinkles above your head.

"I did it, Mum," you whisper.

You have fulfilled your quest.

Turn to **400**.

208

The hooded figure takes off in pursuit, and as you pound down the hill the footfalls behind you keep pace. You realise that escape is impossible – even if you reach The Tangles, you won't have time to hide. You must turn and fight.

If you have the HATCHET, turn to **154**.

If you don't, turn to **271**.

"Interesting," a voice mutters. It seems to come from the walls themselves. "The child shows some intelligence."

The chamber starts to spin, the walls close in. You feel the same dizziness that you felt as you approached the first chamber. In fact, you are in that first chamber. You get up, not sure why you were lying down, and see that the creature has gone. In its place stands a frail old woman with wild white hair, leaning on a cane.

"Why are you here?" she asks in a dry, eggshell voice.

You tell her that you're looking for an alchemist who lived in your mother's hall, and the effect is instant.

"What was your mother's name?"

"Idriel."

"Prove it."

If you'd like to show her your LOCKET, turn to **110**.

If you'd prefer to show her the BOOK OF FAIRY TALES, turn to **304**.

210

You decline the old man's offer as politely as you can, and he gives a haughty sniff and shuffles from the room. You'd swear that his fur collar squeaked at you as he passed. After checking that all your items are still in your satchel, you swing down from the hammock, but as you near the door, someone hobbles across to block your exit.

"Where do you think you're going, my young cuttlefish?"

An old pirate with a peg leg jabs his cutlass at your satchel and weapon.

"Why don't you leave them 'ere with me and swim on your way?"

His laugh turns into a hacking cough and sours his mood.

If you'd like to give him Flynt and all your items, turn to **303**.

If you want to fight your way past him, turn to **86**.

211

Pustula lies thrashing and cursing at your feet, his cord to the demon severed. Gucifer has never known pain like it! With an anguished roar the creature dives underwater. Pustula rolls down his throat with a cry, and you grab hold of a tooth to avoid following him. In the pitch dark, you begin to stab. It must feel like a flea bite to a creature this size, but you hack and slash at any piece of flesh you can reach. The heat and the stench are overpowering. Stars burst in front of your eyes and the tooth slips from your grasp...

When you open your eyes, the stars are still there. But these ones are different. These ones are real. You hear Gucifer's moan, far away, receding into the depths. He's left you floating on the waves. A piece of driftwood nudges you in the side and you grab hold. That's the last you remember.

Gain 1 ABILITY point and turn to **255**.

A thick, tattooed arm reaches out and pulls you inside. A spluttering candle is shoved under your face, and the man bends down and peers at you from beneath a pair of dark, shaggy eyebrows.

"This way," he says. And you follow him through the bar room and into the kitchen. Here he lights a lamp. Without saying a word, he stokes the stove and cracks a couple of eggs into a pan. He takes a kettle off the hob and pours you a mug of steaming tea. It's not until you've eaten your eggs that he sits down opposite.

"What brings you here, Rowan?"

And so you tell him all that's happened since you were woken in the night, and also Old Joe's advice. When you've finished he refills your mug. Only then does he say anything more.

"Many people stop here at the Cat and Coracle. People from beyond our borders. And they bring rumours of a dark force gathering. They say the shadow grows, but cannot explain what they mean."

He sighs.

"Their ways of speaking are foreign, but their fear is real."

He looks at you closely, and his eyes glow in the lamplight.

"I know how to find most people in Helmsgard. Even those who would normally stay hidden. Wait here a moment."

He leaves the room and you sip the strong tea. When the innkeeper returns he's holding a silver bracelet set with a green stone.

"Wear this and go to the market tomorrow," he says. "Look for Madoc the mapmaker."

He smiles sadly and ruffles your hair.

"You've had a long night, for one so young. Rest here awhile, before you go on your way."

Add a SILVER BRACELET to your LOG BOOK, and add 2 LIFE points.

Then, if you have a WHITE FLOWER, turn to **384**.

If you don't, turn to **136**.

213

With your eyes as wide and innocent as a fawn's, you tell the alchemist that you found the broken chain lying on the ground, and picked it up because you liked the colour.

The alchemist eyes you suspiciously, then turns away. You wipe away a bead of sweat that was just about to trickle down your brow.

Turn to **119**.

214

Pressed against the cliff, you have to rely more on sight than feel as you climb down. Eventually you make it onto the narrow dock with your limbs shaking, but attached to your body, at least.

Turn to **220**.

215

The footfalls behind you get louder and louder, and you realise you cannot escape. Even if you gain The Tangles, you'll have no time to hide. Slowly, wearily, you come to a stop and turn around. Your pursuers have stopped, too, waiting to see what you do.

If you decide to fight these four armed pursuers, turn to **230**.

If you conclude that the odds are stacked too far against you, turn to **107**.

216

The alchemist's laboratory lies beneath the sewers of Helmsgard, and the only route you know is through the old docklands. Keeping to the shaded side of the street, you set off. The city looks fresher than you remember. Broken cobbles have been replaced and graffiti scrubbed away. Newly cut timber is stacked by the old blacksmith's, which burnt down years ago.

You hear the rumbling of cart wheels and step aside. Horses round the bend, sweating under the weight of their load. They're followed by a huge iron cage, flanked by two guards and filled with prisoners. The women wear the patterned headscarf seen in the eastern regions of the kingdom. The men have beards. The children huddle close to parents who can no longer protect them.

Your eye falls on a man with thick, tattooed arms and dark eyebrows. He's staring at you intently and your mouth drops open. It's the innkeeper from the Cat and Coracle! The man Joe formed the watch with before the invasion. The man he told you to trust over the city guards. He must have escaped Helmsgard and gone east, where they captured him at last. Your hand reaches for Flynt but his eyes open wide. He mouths the word 'no'. You hesitate and look at the two guards.

If you'd like to attack them and try to free the prisoners, turn to **351**.

If you decide to let the wagon pass, turn to **22**.

217

The guard is twice your size, and each time you parry his attack it nearly knocks you off your feet. You're not sure how much longer you can keep him at bay. He raises his mace, but the blow never comes. A look of surprise spreads slowly across his face, and he topples to earth with a thud. Behind him stands a man with a broken staff. His eyes are bright grey. He drops the staff and holds up his wrist. You see a silver bracelet with a green stone – and the stone is glowing. You look at your own bracelet and let out a gasp. Yours is glowing too.

"Come with me," he says. "Quickly."

Turn to **355**.

218

With one final look at the stone doors, you head back to the cliff face. Slowly you make your way up and over the ridge, until you see Heston, fishing off the bow of the ship.

"No luck?" he calls, as you trudge across the shingle.

You shake your head.

"What now, then?"

You stare out to sea.

"Can you get us to the Lonely Isle from here?"

He nods and calls back.

"We should leave while the tide's in."

As you sail away, a single thought whispers: 'are you too late?'

Heston does what he can to make up for lost time. His cough gets worse through the night, but under his orders you learn how to work the ropes and sail into the wind. By the evening of the second day you once again see the Lonely Isle on the horizon.

Turn to **431**.

219

Nettle nods slowly and points down a path that leads even deeper into the forest. Ancient trees hem it in on either side, with only the odd shard of sunlight piercing the gloom.

"Did I mention she was old?" she asks. "She was old when Old Man Tree was just a sapling. Compared to her we're alive for the blink of an eye. If she takes an interest, she'll give you a chance to meet her. But watch your step, because she likes her little games, yes she does."

If you'd like to set off along this path, turn to **81**.

If you'd like to change your mind and return to Helmsgard, turn to **421**.

If you'd like to ask Nettle to come with you to meet the Old Lady of the Forest, turn to **202**.

220

In front of you stands an entrance of curious design:
a sliding gateway set in front of a pair of solid stone
doors. The gates are wrought from some kind
of dark metal, and they're already open.
Beyond are the doors. Two great, grey slabs
of rock – completely blank, except for

a thin crack that shows where they meet.
But there's no sign of a lock. You step back. Surely
you must be able to open them from the outside?

If you work out how, turn to the entry
you find.

If you can't find it, turn to **118**.

The hooded stranger fights in silence. His expression never changes, even as he strikes the fatal blow. Madoc charges through the doorway and sees you fall. With a great cry he leaps forward, and the hooded man crumples under the ferocity of his onslaught. But it's too late. Madoc lifts you up and runs outside.

"Hold on, Rowan," he gasps, running through the streets with you in his arms.

The rooftops jump and shudder in your vision, and you see that the sky has cleared. The stars are out.

Then they start to fade.

'Why are they doing that?' you wonder sleepily.

It's your last thought.

222

"Not quite. Creeval still has his shadow."

Deduct 1 ABILITY point and turn to **404**.

223

Something yanks hard at the bait and you grab your reel. The pole bends almost double under the strain.

"Let 'im out or your line will snap!" shouts Stumpy. "You have to tire 'im first."

So you let the line out, and it's only when it starts to slow that you make your move. Every muscle in your arm screams as you reel in your catch.

"It's a speartail!" shouts Stumpy, stamping his wooden leg in excitement. "You've caught a speartail! Ain't none of us'll beat that 'un!"

Together, you haul the huge fish aboard.

Gain 1 ABILITY point, then turn to **52**.

224

You dart into a warren of narrow lanes and damp passageways. A stranger would soon be lost, but every twist and turn you make brings you closer to Madoc's cottage. It's not long before you reach an empty square with a tree at the centre. Its shadow stands black against the dusty ground, and as you approach, one of its branches starts to move. Strange. There's no wind. And the tree itself is still... You stop dead. The long finger of shadow has almost reached your boots. Leaping back, you fumble for your shadow blade.

SHADOW WRAITH

Rounds: 4   Damage: 4

YOU

Leather armour doesn't work against shadow wraiths, so you can't use a defence bonus in this fight.

If you win, turn to **152**.

If you lose, turn to **261**.

225

You struggle from Joe's grasp and roll off the mattress. He stands between you and the ladder. Grey-haired, sleeves rolled up, smelling of sawdust. Smelling like he always did. The only family you've ever known and he's been taken from you. Rage wells up, tightening your chest, but suddenly Joe lunges across the mattress and gives you no time to think.

Roll one DICE and add it to your SKILL and ATHLETICISM levels.

If your total is 17 or higher, turn to **283**.

If it's 16 or lower, turn to **189**.

226

As you raise the water, the leaves of the old tree shiver, but you're too thirsty to take much notice. The water touches your lips and the whole tree creaks and groans. You feel something snake around your ankles. Roots are pushing up through the ground, coiling round and round until you're lifted high in the air and only your head is free to move.

"Oh dear, oh dear," laughs the imp. "You are up to your neck, aren't you?"

If you want to plead for help, turn to **357**.

If you want to try to free yourself from the tree, turn to **285**.

227

"Storm approaching off the starboard quarter!" Betty Bottle shouts.

You turn to see dark clouds blocking out the sun. They stretch from the sea to the sky like a colossal wave.

"Where's that come from?" Casper mutters.

Lightning pulses in the clouds and a thick mist engulfs the ship.

"Lower the sails!" the captain roars.

As the crew rush to the ropes, you see lights floating through the mist. Torches. A giant galley takes shape. On either side are rowers stripped to the waist, and in between, dark forms roam the deck. But where are the people casting these shadows? You can't see them. And suddenly the ship alters its course...

"BRACE!" shouts the captain.

The galley rams into your trawler with a sickening crunch. Then they stream aboard, those dark shapes that stretch and glide like things from a nightmare. Stumpy is the first to fall, harpooning thin air and going quiet and stiff as the shadow creeps up his body. He falls awkwardly to the floor, his wooden leg clattering against the deck.

"What are these things?" yells Betty Bottle.

"How do you fight 'em?" roars Captain Hamshanks.

"You can't!" shouts Casper. "Just don't let them touch you!"

Add together your SIXTH SENSE and SKILL levels.

If your total is 11 or higher, turn to **347**.

If it's 10 or lower, turn to **424**.

228

Your aim is as good as your luck – all six marsh goblins are snared by your net. They writhe and snarl in a spiky yet harmless heap.

Gain 1 ABILITY point, then turn to **157**.

229

Deduct 1 ABILITY point.

With your mind perhaps scrambled by the bizarre sight looming over the ship, you answer the creature's question truthfully. He clasps his hands together in delight.

"Then you are the person to whom we were instructed to render our services!"

Gucifer gives a great roar, and the tentacles around the ship flex and twist.

"Yes, Gucifer is pleased too. Although, all things considered, his interest in your name is moot..."

You ask who gave them this task.

Turn to **390**.

230

Your bravery is outmatched only by your foolishness. There's no way you can beat four full-grown, armed opponents. After a brief but painful struggle, you are bound and gagged and a sack is pulled over your head. Then you're carried away like a lamb for market.

Deduct 2 LIFE points, and if you had a HATCHET, delete it from your LOG BOOK. Then turn to **94**.

231

You're driven back, catch your heel on a loose cobble and fall hard. Without a flicker of emotion, your opponent raises his arm for the fatal blow. Then his mouth opens in surprise. Slowly, he sags to the ground, revealing the boy behind, sheathing his cutlass.

You gasp your thanks and look around for the second man. He lies in a heap nearby. The boy is glaring down at you.

"Didn't I tell you not to go this way? I should have left you to it."

As you look up at him, your eyes widen in recognition.

"Casper?"

"How did you... Rowan?"

He holds out his hand to help you to your feet, and you're about to speak when he interrupts.

"Wait. First we get off the streets, then we talk."

He leads you down to the docks and onto a large fishing trawler.

Deduct 2 LIFE points, then turn to **305**.

232

Creeval shakes his head and sighs.

"No, Rowan. Have you not seen the shadows without a body?"

Deduct 1 ABILITY point, and turn to **336**.

233

"Whole-Harlan was purified."

Your attempted smile fades, and you ask what he means.

"Whole-Harlan was purified."

Clearly he's not willing, or able, to say any more.

If you want to ask another question, turn to **111**.

If you decide you've heard enough, turn to **12**.

234

"Only the Guardian can open the door to the chamber of the Flame. The fuel that feeds the Flame lasts for one hundred years. If it's not replaced the Flame goes out and the kingdom lies unprotected. That's when He'll make his move. The prophecy says that an army of darkness will descend on Arkendale. Our defences will fall and greatest warriors falter. Chaos reigns, crops wither in the field... and out of this He will come, offering peace and prosperity."

She looks up with a strange smile.

"And all that He'll ask in return is your free will. He will make you into slaves, and you will let him."

She pauses.

"All this will happen if the Flame goes out. THAT is why they came for you, Rowan. The hundred years are nearly up. The Flame's power is failing, and the Guardian's time is upon us."

She stops, and suddenly her stern face softens. You can almost see tenderness there.

"But I thought you were dead. All my experiments – my attempts to create a creature that could fight the coming dark – they were born of despair. Yet here you are – in the one place you needed to be. And He has driven you here. His fear of you has given us our chance. We must take it. Come with me."

She hobbles over to a bookcase and pushes two books into the wall. There's a loud click and the case swings forward to reveal a narrow doorway. She mutters a few words and the tip of her cane glows as you follow her down a dark stairway.

Turn to **399**.

235

You manage to slam the hatch shut just in time. Breathing a sigh of relief, you turn to leave the stone chamber and make your way back to the junction.

Turn to **165**.

236

STREET URCHIN

Rounds: 2   Damage: 1

YOU

If you win, turn to **23**.

If you lose, turn to **173**.

237

Almost at once you find yourself at the forest's edge. You turn around in surprise, but the path has disappeared. When you finally walk back through Helmsgard's East gate, the sun is in your eyes and Owen the gatekeeper has been replaced by the afternoon shift. You don't recognise the new guard, and there's something unnerving about the way he looks at you. But he lets you pass unhindered.

If you'd like to visit the market straight away, turn to **331**.

If you'd first like to report your attempted kidnapping to the City Guard, turn to **200**.

If you'd like to go back to the workshop, to see if Old Joe has returned, turn to **377**.

238

You wait for the cart to pass, then make your move.

Roll one DICE and add it to your ATHLETICISM level.

If your total is 10 or higher, turn to **345**.

If it's 9 or lower, turn to **4**.

239

As the wraith fades with a mournful cry, you see the guard turn and run. He'll return soon with reinforcements. In any case, the cart is long gone. You turn and hurry towards the old docks.

Turn to **187**.

240

The old man bows and accepts your item.

"You see this, my beauties? This is cheese for you and a bottle for me!"

You leave the inn and make your way to the docks.

Turn to **78**.

241

You wake in a vast cavern. You are strapped to a post, and your hair hangs about your shoulders in lank, matted strands. It's as if you've been unconscious for a long, long time. A bright light shines from high above, casting your shadow onto some kind of metal disc. It's inscribed with rings of strange markings that start to glow and rotate. From the far side of the chamber, you hear a familiar, festering laugh. Something flashes across the disc and darkness descends. Your adventure is over.

242

"Madoc?" he says. "Who's that, then?"

You tell him the only thing you know – that he's a mapmaker.

"Well if it's a map you're after, there's a man here that sells 'em. You've just missed him, but he'll be at the Weeping Willow with all the others. I'd take you there meself, but I got other plans."

He spits on the cobbles and continues on his way. You call after him and ask what the man looks like.

"He looks like a mapmaker!" he shouts. "Looks just like what he is!"

The Weeping Willow is a tavern near the town square. It's where the traders go to spend the money they've earned, and then money they haven't. Normally you'd avoid the place, but right now it's your only option.

Turn to **15**.

243

Your instincts whisper that you should stay in the procession and not draw attention to yourself. You take a deep breath and carry on.

Turn to **85**.

244

Your arm is quick and your aim is true – the war hammer strikes Woad between his shoulder blades. He staggers on a few more paces then sinks to the floor. You drag his body into a side street, and just as you're about to leave you see something shiny under his cloak. It's a city guard's badge. He's too young to have one of those, but if it's found on his body it would start a major search. You hide it under your tunic.

Add a CITY GUARD'S BADGE to your LOG BOOK.

If you'd like to continue on to the workshop, turn to **344**.

If you'd like to turn back and head for the market, turn to **55**.

If you decide that now is the time to report your attempted kidnapping to the City Guard, turn to **200**.

245

Your shot hits Cork-eared Karl on the forehead with a satisfying splat. His mouth falls open in shock as the gunge dribbles down his nose. Then his face goes red, his eyes screw shut and he tips back his head and wails like a child.

"It's not fair!" he bawls in a high, whiny voice.

You open your mouth to laugh, but find it suddenly filled with something gooey and bitter. Jonas shouts in triumph. Karl is right – it is so unfair. Why is Jonas such a big meanie?

And now all the crew are laughing at you, too. Even Casper, who you thought was your bestest friend in the whole world! You sit down on the deck with your legs crossed and suck your thumb between loud wails.

Deduct 1 ABILITY point, then turn to **52**.

246

You wish the boy would step out of the shadows. Perhaps he's being cautious. But you also remember the advice to stick to the main roads.

If you'd like to follow that advice, turn to **180**.

If you'd like to ignore the advice and walk down the dark lane, turn to **97**.

247

Creeval raises his hands.

"If that is your wish."

He makes a complex pattern in the air and the symbols light up. Slowly, the rings begin to turn. Each symbol moves into line with Casper's shadow, until the machine comes to rest with a final clank. The symbols pulse four times and fade. Casper looks up. Then suddenly he drops onto the Dial. For a moment you're not sure what's happened, but slowly he gets to his feet. You've released him! Gain 1 ABILITY point.

If the crew are with you in the chamber, turn to **45**.

If they're not, turn to **122**.

248

You cry out in pain – you've been bitten by a rat. Deduct 1 LIFE point. Then you come to a crossroads. If you want to go:

North, turn to **333**.　　　　　South, turn to **397**.

East, turn to **9**.　　　　　　West, turn to **204**.

249

Your pursuers are gaining fast. You slip down a passage and onto a broad street that runs uphill towards the market square. With not a moment to lose, you must choose between three options.

If you decide to head to a City Guard station on the market square, turn to **196**.

If you choose to hide in the stables across the street, turn to **67**.

If you want to turn down the street to an area of the city called The Tangles, turn to **293**.

250

The tunnel bends towards the mountain at the head of the inlet, and is lit by torches that flicker with green flame. Eventually, you come to a fork. The left-hand path gives off a chill that can be felt even through the freezing air of the main tunnel. Its walls are made entirely of ice. From the right-hand path, two voices reach your ears.

If you'd like to head down the icy path to the left, turn to **158**.

If you'd prefer to take the right-hand path, turn to **32**.

251

A young guard lunges at you wildly, but you're too quick and he's too clumsy. Leaping to one side you give him a shove to help him on his way. He flies into the table of traders and scatters their drinks. The tavern goes quiet as the huge butcher slowly, almost thoughtfully, wipes beer from his face.

"Here," he says, in a voice that sounds like it could saw through bone. "This must be yours."

He picks up the young guard and launches him back towards his comrades.

"No one does that to a guard!" one of them shouts.

Tankards are slammed down and mouths wiped on the backs of sleeves. Madoc grabs you by the arm.

"Come on," he says.

You duck to let an empty flagon fly over your head. As the two of you make for the door, you see the butcher dunking a guard headfirst into a cauldron of chicken broth.

"Where's your bracelet?" Madoc asks, once you're on the street. "That was to show me you were in trouble."

As you both race away from the Weeping Willow, you tell him how you lost it.

Turn to **355**.

252

You have no choice but to fight the guard.

PRISON GUARD

Rounds: 4   Damage: 2

If you win, turn to **371**.

If you lose, turn to **93**.

253

You fire into the sky. Jonas and Karl look at you in confusion, then they look at each other. They've both realised the same thing at the same time: the threat to Karl is Jonas, and the threat to Jonas is Karl! As one, they swing their gungers around, and reel backwards with gunge dripping from their faces. They glower at each other and growl. But the growls soon turn to whimpers and wails.

"What did you do that for?" Karl cries.

"You did it first!" shouts Jonas, stamping his foot.

The two of them run at each other with windmilling arms, then collapse to the deck and bawl for their mummies. The rest of the crew roar with laughter and Captain Hamshanks points her horn towards you with a flourish.

"Rowan wins!" she cries. "Well, blow me down!"

Casper rushes across to congratulate you.

"Did you miss on purpose?" he asks, wide-eyed.

Suddenly you feel a heavy hand on your shoulder. Captain Hamshanks holds out the item you gave her as payment.

"There's more to you than meets the eye, Rowan. I hope you find what you're looking for."

Gain 2 ABILITY points, add the item back into your LOG BOOK, then turn to **52**.

254

"That's the symbol of the Guardians of the Flame!" Madoc whispers. "They say there's an oak that's older than the kingdom itself, standing in a place that no longer exists. They say it's the location of the Flame. I'd always thought it was an old wives' tale."

He looks at you with his bright grey eyes. "Perhaps I was wrong."

You return the look in silence. Suddenly, your head starts to spin. The men in hoods, your mother, and now this talk of the 'Guardians of the Flame'... You stumble away from the book.

Roll one DICE.

If your score is 4 or over, turn to **130**.

If it's 3 or under, turn to **292**.

255

"Choose a card, Rowan."

You hear birdsong and smell flowers on the breeze. Your clothes are dry and the grass between your fingers is warm. You open your eyes. A shimmering green light slowly comes into focus and you find yourself lying beneath a broad tree.

"Choose a card."

You sit up. At your feet is a pool, and on the other side stands a woman with short, dark hair. She's dressed in a yellow robe and in her hands are a pack of cards. She draws one and throws it face-up onto the water. As you get to your feet, you see that you're in a walled garden, with roses growing up the ancient stonework.

"Where am I?" you ask.

"The same place you were," she replies. "Before the waters came. Choose a card."

There are now twelve cards floating in the dark pool. As you step closer, you see stars reflected in the water, as if it were night-time.

"Who are you?"

"Rowan, you are dying. Look at the cards. You must tell them what you want. Pick the three that will take you home."

You stare at the cards and start to shiver, despite the sunlight in the garden.

"You haven't much time. Your body is failing."

The birds still sing, but they seem farther off, and you can hear waves all around you.

"I don't even know where my home is anymore," you say.

She doesn't reply, yet somehow in that silence your mind clears.

"It's not where..." she begins, as if reading your thoughts.

"...It's who," you whisper, your eyes wide.

Old Joe. The man who took you in when you were helpless and became your home one fateful night, long ago. You look again at the cards.

"They are for you alone," the woman says. "Only you can read them."

Turn the page to see the cards. When you have chosen the three cards that contain the clearest clues to Old Joe, add their numbers together, and turn to that entry.

If you chose incorrectly, turn to **163**.

256

The crates are heavy and you'll have to open them on the cart. They're stacked in three lines, all unmarked. You pick up a crowbar, and look from one crate to the next.

If you'd like to open a crate from the left line, turn to **302**.

If you'd like to open a crate from the middle line, turn to **71**.

If you'd like to open a crate from the right line, turn to **359**.

257

You dig the caltrops from your bag and scatter them on the ground behind you. But the goblins are small and nimble and jink through with no trouble at all.

Delete the CALTROPS from your LOG BOOK, then turn to **198**.

258

Trees creak and groan as you make your way along the dark path. You hear a faint cry. In the moonlight you make out a figure lying in the centre of a large hollow to your left.

"Help me!" the figure cries weakly.

It sounds like a boy's voice, maybe someone the same age as you. You can't make out his face, but he waves at you slowly. You call and ask if he's hurt.

"Help me!" he says again.

If you'd like to help, turn to **168**.

If you decide to hurry on to Port Darktide, turn to **35**.

259

Madoc goes into another room and comes back with the parchment. It's soft with age, and discoloured by blood. Slowly, carefully, you unroll it and see a message written in a flowing hand.

"I've read the message, and can make nothing of it," Madoc adds. "But maybe it will mean something to you."

You read it over several times. At first there seems no sense in the message at all, but then something stirs, a memory so close that it's like your mother's whisper in your ear.

"I know where to look," you say. "She's telling me where to look."

If you've already been back to Old Joe's workshop, turn to **148**.

If you haven't, turn to **39**.

260

You drag Owen's body into a dark passage, cursing the Shadow Reaper with a hatred you've never felt before. As you walk the short distance left to Madoc's, you promise vengeance.

Turn to **379**.

261

The shadow blade drops from your frozen grasp. The wraith was too fast and too deadly. You wonder whose it was. Perhaps someone you knew. Helmsgard fades around you as your quest ends back where it all began.

A ripple rolls through the entire hollow. You look around in confusion as the ground falls away and a pit appears beneath your feet. The stench of rotting flesh and death rises. Too late you realise the figure was a lure! You've stumbled into the mouth of some monstrous burrowing creature that feasts on foolish travellers. With a despairing cry, you plunge into its gullet.

Turn to **197**.

263

A faint, deep growl makes the candle on the table quiver. The alchemist ushers you out of the laboratory and up to the sewers. Another growl sends the rats squealing for their holes. There at the crossroads lies a dark shape, with huge golden eyes.

"Good boy, Wowl. Easy now."

The creature whines softly and rests its head on its paws. It's the biggest wolf you've ever seen, and folded over its black flanks are a pair of grey wings.

"Part-wolf, part-owl," the alchemist cries triumphantly.

She pats it on the muzzle.

"Come on, boy. Up we go."

The creature places its nose under her foot and lifts her gently onto its back. She looks down impatiently.

"Time is not our friend, Rowan."

You scramble up behind her and Wowl leaps forward. The walls of the sewer pass by in a blur and daylight appears up ahead. With a last bound, you burst through the opening and soar up over the rooftops of Helmsgard. The alchemist turns.

"It will be nightfall before we reach the coast, you should rest. Drink this."

She hands you a small vial filled with a few drops of something bitter. Fields and hillsides flash by beneath you, but despite the speed and the cold wind, your eyelids droop. You rest your head in Wowl's soft fur, just for a moment...

Roll one DICE and add the number to your LIFE points. Remember, you can have a maximum of 12.

Turn to **341**.

264

This guard is highly trained, and her chain moves in a grey blur. If you roll a double and lose the round, subtract double the damage.

TEMPLE GUARD

Rounds: 6   Damage: 2

YOU

If you win, turn to **188**.

If you lose, turn to **147**.

265

You leap from the cart as half-Harlan lunges forwards. You're quick, but not quite quick enough, and feel a sharp pain across the back of your thigh. Landing with a grimace, you call out for help and yell that you've been kidnapped.

Deduct 2 LIFE points and turn to **44**.

266

The wind's set fair and the crew unfurl the sails and sail out with the tide. Once you're clear of the port, Captain Hamshanks orders the crew to grab their fishing rods.

"Fattest fish for the captain's table – and you seapups can fight over the rest!" she roars.

Casper teaches you how to cast a line, and soon you're sending your bait arching over the waves with an expert arm. Roll one DICE to see what you catch.

If you roll a 1, turn to **312**.

If you roll a 2, turn to **223**.

If you roll a 3, turn to **274**.

If you roll 4-6, turn to **164**.

267

"She was your mother, too," you say in a voice half-strangled.

Shadow veils your brother's face once more. The pale eyes glitter like ice.

"She was a fool. She could have been the greatest Guardian there's ever been. She could have pushed back Arkendale's borders until they reached the edges of the Earth."

"With your help," you say softly, almost to yourself.

"Yes. With my help. Is that so bad?"

He sweeps his staff in a wide arc.

"I've brought order to chaos. Prosperity where there was none."

"By creating a kingdom of slaves!" you cry.

"They accepted my help."

"You gave them no choice."

The two of you stare at each other across the chamber, your brother's face flickering in and out like lightning in a storm cloud.

"But you've made yours, brother."

He points his staff, and raises an evil-looking war hammer.

If you have a YELLOW POUCH, turn to **88**.

If not, turn to **413**.

268

As you struggle to your feet, the alchemist notices the red chain tied to your belt.

"Where did you find that?" she cries.

If you want to tell her the truth, turn to **7**.

If you don't, turn to **213**.

269

You turn to run as the shadow slides into the chamber. But you've seen how quickly those things move and know you won't get far.

If you have the SILVER RING, turn to **385**.

If not, turn to **77**.

270

You catch a glimpse of the boy disappearing down the street and take off after him, weaving through the crowd like an alley cat. Finally you grab him by the arm. It's nothing but skin and bone. He looks like a cornered animal, and you realise two things. One: he definitely has your bracelet, and two: the money he'd get for that bracelet would feed him for a month.

If you'd like to fight him for the bracelet, turn to **236**.

If you decide to let him go, turn to **344**.

271

Your bravery is unquestionable, but some situations are hopeless. As you turn towards the hooded figure, the slope of the street makes him look even taller than he really is. Drawing his weapon, he backs you up against the wall and waits for his companions to arrive. Soon you are bound and gagged, and a sack is pulled over your head. You're carried away in the dark.

Turn to **94**.

272

Flynt is sent spinning from your exhausted grasp. The fight is over and you have lost. Lord Creeval calls down from across the cavern.

"Watch, Rowan. Witness your fate."

His head tilts back and he intones in a strange language.

Turn to **411**.

273

You can't turn back without attracting attention, so there's no choice but to carry on into the square. Heart pounding, not daring to look, you pass the guard. Any moment you're expecting him to shout 'HALT!' – but no shout comes. With a sigh of relief you look around the square. That's when a heavy hand clamps down on your shoulder.

"I think you'd better come with me."

You twist around and see the guard standing behind you. He pulls a mace from his belt.

CITY GUARD

Rounds: 6   Damage: 2

YOU

If you're carrying the SILVER BRACELET and survive
four rounds, turn to **217**.

If you're not carrying the bracelet, you'll have to fight to
the finish.

If you win, turn to **124**.

If you lose, turn to **378**.

You feel something tug on your bait and eagerly reel in your catch. A dark shape appears beneath the surface.

You look over to Casper and ask excitedly what it is.

Slowly, the shape gets larger. You shout for someone to grab a net as it breaks the surface, glossy and black... and made entirely of leather.

The crew roars with laughter.

"Rowan's cort 'is dinner!" yells Cork-eared Karl.

"Looks a bit t-t-tough!" says Shiverin' Shaun.

You give them a proud stare and throw the boot back overboard.

Deduct 1 ABILITY point, then turn to **52**.

The buildings get smaller as you near Madoc's cottage. You turn down a quiet lane and see a guard heading towards you. He's broad-shouldered and tall, with the same blank stare as everyone else. That's why it takes a moment for you to recognise him... It's Owen the gatekeeper. He's known you since you were a child, and used to bring a rabbit or two for Old Joe if he'd been out hunting. Maybe a treat for you. But now there's not a flicker of emotion on his face as the two of you near. If you don't get past him without arousing suspicion, you'll have to fight one of your oldest friends.

Keeping your head perfectly straight, your face blank, you glance down to check that your shadow is hidden.

Roll one DICE and add it to your SKILL level.

If your total is 11 or higher, turn to **178**.

If it's 10 or lower, turn to **18**.

276

You reason that you've done nothing wrong, and therefore have nothing to fear. There'll be a perfectly reasonable explanation for all this, you tell yourself, as you climb down the ladder from the platform where you sleep. In fact, it's probably a set-up by your friends, trying to scare you because they know Old Joe is away. He's the carpenter who's raised you as his own. Yes, that must be it! You grin as you unbolt the door. And then you meet those sightless eyes, that somehow seem to see more than yours ever could, and your grin freezes in place. Two of the hooded figures pin your arms behind your back.

"So, Rowan," the man sighs, almost sadly. "After all this time you answer the door like a common servant."

His voice hardens.

"The rope!"

You are bound and gagged and a sack is pulled over your head. That same festering laugh seems to creep from all sides as you're carried away from your home.

Turn to **94**.

277

You throw yourself backwards, but not quite quickly enough. A heavy blow knocks the breath from your chest. You scrabble to your feet and back away from the door. A man follows you out, mace hanging loose in his hand. Then another man emerges. And another...

Deduct 2 LIFE points and turn to **36**.

278

You turn to watch Helmsgard disappearing behind you. The old docks, the smoking furnaces, the workshop, somewhere down there among the rooftops. And above it all the Black Tower, glowering like a dark sentinel. Three shapes seem to circle its heights, but when you blink they're gone. A shiver runs down your spine, and you turn away. Over the horizon lies Port Darktide, and beyond that, the Lonely Isle.

You hunker down into Wowl's thick fur as the wind whistles past, and your thoughts return to the alchemist's message. So, the Flame can be relit. What then? Does Joe get his shadow back? Maybe you've killed it already. Doubt gnaws at your heart as you see again his blank, lifeless eyes... but suddenly a primeval screech rips through the air. Three creatures are climbing towards you, their giant, bat-like wings glowing red in the sun. Wowl snarls as they soar by to cruise the high currents, effortlessly keeping pace with your flight.

If you have a bow and arrows, turn to **393**.

If you don't, turn to **38**.

On a cramped street lined with sagging timber buildings you find a hostel that's open at this late hour. The man at the bar brings you a bowl of spicy fish stew, and when you've finished he shows you into a long, windowless room lit by a single oil lamp. Hammocks are slung from the low ceiling, and the walls are damp with the snores of a dozen sleepers. You secure your satchel to your leg before stowing it at the end of your hammock, then close your aching eyes.

Add 5 LIFE points, then turn to **335**.

280

If you'd like to open a crate from the left line, turn to **426**.

If you'd like to open a crate from the middle line, turn to **307**.

If you'd like to open a crate from the right line, turn to **149**.

281

Gripping Flynt, you advance to meet your brother. He flickers between his body and his shadow, and you can't be sure whether your weapon will hurt him. So after every successful attack, roll one DICE. If you roll a 4-6, your strike was successful and you can deduct his COMBAT points as normal. But if you roll a 1-3, FLYNT passes right through his shadow and you cannot deduct any COMBAT points.

SHADOW REAPER

Rounds: 8   Damage: 4

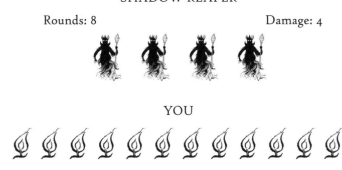

YOU

Leather armour doesn't work against the Shadow Reaper. You can only use a defence bonus if you have a CHAINMAIL VEST. Also, if he still has his staff, whenever you roll a double you're hit by a purple bolt, and must deduct 1 LIFE point regardless of whether you win or lose the round.

If you win, turn to **26**.

If you lose, turn to **391**.

282

A boy with rags for clothes and no shoes at all bumps into you.

"Sorry your honour. It being so busy..." he says, grasping your hands and shaking them earnestly.

You carry on, absentmindedly rubbing your wrist. Suddenly you stop dead. The silver bracelet has gone! You spin around. Might that boy have slipped it from you?

Delete the SILVER BRACELET from your LOG BOOK.

If you have an ENDURANCE level of 5 or above, turn to **270**.

If you have an ENDURANCE level of 4 or below, turn to **98**.

283

In one smooth move, you spin away from his outstretched arms and leap from the platform. But it's a big drop and you jar your ankle slightly as you land.

Deduct 1 LIFE point, then turn to **76**.

284

You walk slowly up to the hatch. Flakes of rust drift to your feet as you wrench it aside. Heart thumping, you peer through the opening. You see a cavern, lit by a huge green flame burning high above. Dark shapes flit around the vast, empty space. As your eyes adjust you see more and more of them. Hundreds, thousands, it's impossible to tell.

Suddenly one of the shadows stops and turns – as if it's looking right at you. Then it lunges towards the hatch.

Roll one DICE.

If you roll 1-3, turn to **396**.

If you roll 4-6, turn to **235**.

285

You wriggle and squirm, but the roots don't give an inch. In fact, they tighten further, until you're gasping for breath. All around you, the leaves shiver and hiss. Deduct 2 LIFE points.

"Quiet, now, Old Man Tree," the imp calls out in a high voice. "The young ones are sometimes the least stupid. Let's give them one last chance, shall we?"

Slowly, with a disappointed creak, the roots loosen a little.

"Now then, my little thief, what have you got to say for yourself?" she asks.

If you want to apologise for taking the water, turn to **162**.

If you want to try one more time to free yourself, turn to **31**.

286

The three guards fan out and advance.

If you have CALTROPS and would like to use them, turn to **117**.

If you don't, turn to **129**.

287

Who would have thought the fate of the kingdom would have been decided on the dirty floor of a dingy hostel in Port Darktide? But the pirate's cutlass finds its mark, and you sag into a nearby hammock.

Slowly, it stains red beneath you.

288

Madoc nods.

"Stay close to the door, so they can't cut off your escape. If there's anyone inside, don't fight them – just get out. Do you understand, Rowan? Yes? Good, go."

Your footsteps seem to fill the night with a slow drumbeat. The broken door hangs half-open. You drag it back and step inside. Weak lamplight from the street glints off broken glass, and in the darkness, something shifts.

Roll one DICE and add both your SIXTH SENSE and ATHLETICISM levels.

If your score is 11 or higher, turn to **434**.

If it's 10 or lower, turn to **277**.

Barrels, nets, fishing rods all fall past, but you cling to the mast like a limpet. The sea demon roars and shakes the ship as if it were a toy. Sea and sky tumble one over the other and the mast creaks ominously. But still you hold on... until finally Gucifer tires of his game, and lowers the whole ship into his mouth. It's the moment you've been waiting for. As the tip of the mast disappears down his throat, you roll clear of the deck and onto the creature's soft, purple tongue. In an instant, you have Flynt in your hand and pointed at Pustula.

"If you swallow," you shout, "I'll take him down with me!"

Turn to **102**.

Madoc leads you down to the old docklands. The rotten hulks of old ships loom above the mist rising off the River Wendle. It's low tide, and you climb down a rusting ladder into a passageway between two storehouses. Rats squeak from cracks in the walls as you slip and slide across green stones and rotten driftwood. At the far end is another ladder, leading up to an iron grating. Madoc removes the grating, then climbs back down.

"She won't be easy to find," he says quietly. "Here – take these and try to head towards the centre of the sewers. That's where I heard her incantations, rising up through the pipes."

Add a LANTERN, COMPASS and CHALK to your LOG BOOK.

You ask why he's given you chalk, and he looks past you into the dark tunnel.

"A man stumbled out of here once, saying he'd been lost for many days. Saying the tunnels move. Maybe if you mark every chamber you enter, you'll avoid getting lost... And Rowan."

He grips your arm suddenly.

"People hear all sorts of strange noises at night when it's quiet. They talk about spirits roaming the streets. But I know the alchemist and her experiments."

He releases his grip.

"Just don't give her a reason to dislike you."

You start climbing the ladder, then turn.

"Can you keep watch for Old Joe?" you ask, looking down. "If he sees his workshop and I'm not there..."

"I will, Rowan. I give you my word."

You climb up into the sewer. Stooping to keep your head from scraping the damp bricks, you light your lamp and set off down a long, straight tunnel. You check your compass and see that you're heading northeast. Soon though, your stride starts to falter. The warm air and foul smells are making you dizzy. The compass needle spins around and around...

... Just as your legs start to buckle, the tunnel opens into a high chamber. The air is fresher and you take a few deep breaths. Looking around, you realise you can't find the entrance you came in by. None of them seem to match the compass direction you were following, so you have a choice of four tunnels.

But before you choose, remember Madoc's advice. To avoid going around in circles, 'mark' each chamber you enter by making a note of its entry number in your LOG BOOK.

Now, to go:

North, turn to **306**.

South, turn to **57**.

East, turn to **9**.

West, turn to **204**.

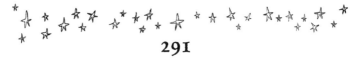

291

No matter how quickly you feint and dodge, the shadow just keeps on coming. Your only thought is to buy some time. A loose rope hangs from the mast, and with a great leap you swing from one end of the ship to the other. You land and roll. On your right, Odan Britches beckons to you from behind a crate and points inside. On your left, you see that the hatch is open to the hold.

If you'd like to run across to Odan Britches, turn to **83**.

If you'd prefer to drop down into the hold, turn to **125**.

A deep-throated purr halts your retreat, and you feel something warm rubbing against your legs. A large tomcat is using your trouser leg to scratch an itch on the back of his head. Madoc walks over, but he seems to be swaying from side to side. In fact, the whole room seems to be swaying like the deck of a ship. He catches you just as the room goes dark.

Turn to **95**.

293

As you pound downhill, the dark entrance to The Tangles jolts and blurs in your vision, and the footfalls of your pursuers get louder in your ear. Looking over your shoulder you see them gaining. You call out for help, but no doors open and no lamps flare.

If your ENDURANCE level is 4 or higher, turn to **311**.

If your ENDURANCE level is 3, turn to **215**.

294

The steps lead to a stone staircase that spirals down the inside of a great, hollow tower. Pale light wavers on the walls, and where the roof should be, you see the moon rippling through the lake.

You pass statues carved from green stone, and at the bottom of the tower, trees stand still in the moonlight. The air is warm and there's a rustle of leaves and flapping of wings. Several passages lead off from the courtyard. One of them has the symbol of a flame carved into its archway, and you feel for the flask inside your satchel. It's still there.

As you pass under the high, wide arch, the birds start to screech. Suddenly the walls light up and a deafening blast throws you to the floor. Water and masonry rain down, tearing off branches and smashing into the courtyard. You peer out as the echoes subside. The lake has gone and a huge dark shape hovers over the tower. Even from down here you see flames flicker from its jaws. A dragon! You thought they'd died out in ancient times.

A voice whispers like a serpent's tongue in your ear.

"There you are, Rowannn. It's been so long..."

Suddenly the beast swoops, and you see something, or someone, on its back. You turn and run through the archway and along the passage. Voices echo all around. Men's, women's, the spirits of Guardians past.

"The Sentinels have awoken, only one square is safe. The Sentinels have awoken, only one square is safe..."

The walls open out on the bend, and you skid to a halt just in time. In front of you is a pit covered by a square grid. You force yourself to take it in. It's nine squares wide by nine squares deep. On the grid stand seven headless statues, each clasping some kind of orb. On the back wall, images suddenly appear in faint, golden lines.

"The Guardian alone sees the lines on the wall. The Guardian shall know on which square to fall."

You hear the screech of the dragon and the crackling of burning trees. The ground shudders and flames lick your heels. It's almost upon you...

Turn over to see the grid and the images on the back wall. When you've found the safe square, count how many in from the left it is, and how many up from the bottom. Put the two numbers together to find its coordinates, and turn to that entry.

If you can't find the safe square, turn to **323**.

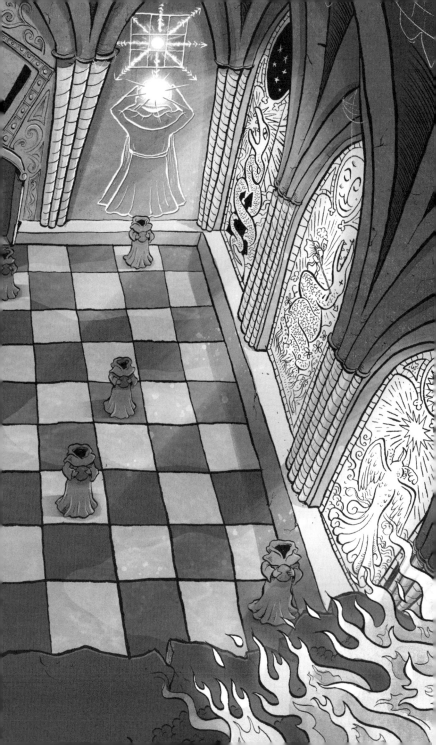

Before leaving the workshop, you close your eyes and take a deep, shuddering breath. So, the spell has transported you home, but somehow a year into the future. The Flame has gone out and Arkendale, or Helmsgard at least, has fallen. Not for the first time, you're fortunate that you haven't got time to take it all in.

You open your eyes and put your hand to the bolt. There are footsteps outside and you wait for them to pass before opening the door. It's a girl you recognise from a street nearby. She's a few years younger than you, and used to play in the alley behind the workshop. Hopscotch, skipping, tag. But now her steps are even and measured, like a teacher's walking into the classroom. And she has no shadow. You look at your own shadow against the door and realise that it won't be long before someone spots it and raises the alarm. That's if Joe doesn't first. You need to get to a safe haven as soon as possible.

If you'd like to make for Madoc's, turn to **43**.

If you'd prefer to head for the alchemist, turn to **216**.

296

If the fuel would affect her, maybe the potion will too... You throw it into the monster's open mouth and stand back.

"That was not the flask, human child."

A tentacle snakes forward and wraps itself around your body, winds its way up and up, and is just about to reach your mouth and nose when it slows to a stop. A vacant look enters the woman's face.

"What wasss that?" she whispers, as the tentacle slips limply from your body.

The monster dissolves before your eyes, droplets raining down upon your upturned face.

Delete the SLEEPING POTION from your LOG BOOK, gain 1 ABILITY point, then turn to **382**.

297

With a desperate cry the shadow drifts away, and you see your brother at last. Older than you by maybe ten, fifteen years. The same hair, the same nose. Different eyes. And as they start to lose their glimmer, he says:

"My name's Ash, by the way."

He tries to laugh, but it ends with a choke.

"You never asked."

And then the glimmer's gone. The body stands, awaiting orders.

Brushing tears angrily from your cheeks, you tell him to leave the chamber, to go wait by the shores of the lake. He obeys without complaint, and you know then that your brother is truly gone.

Turn to **207**.

298

You tie the end of the rope around a rock and lower yourself down the cliff with little trouble.

Delete the ROPE WITH HOOK from your LOG BOOK, then turn to **220**.

299

Nettle sets off at a trot. Following paths known only to her, she makes for Toadflax Dell. At midday you eat handfuls of the mushrooms and nuts that she's foraged. Add 1 LIFE point.

Finally, as the sun is beginning to set, the trees thin out and you reach a shallow hollow at the top of a hill. Down below, Helmsgard is spread before you. The torches are already flickering on the city walls. Nettle stops and points.

"Follow this path across the plain. You see where it starts to curve around the wall? There's a grating at ground level. The middle bar will pull out and you can wriggle through into the alley beyond."

She looks at you strangely.

"Good luck, Rowan."

You call out your thanks, but she's already lost to the trees.

Turn to **75**.

300

You clamber up on deck and Heston follows. The galley pulls away to the north. The clouds and mist have gone, and ahead lies your goal – the Lonely Isle. Somewhere on that grey mass of rock, there burns a flame that must never go out.

Heston looks at you with watery eyes.

"What shall we do, Rowan? I'm an old man, and I'm dying. The choice must be yours."

You move towards him, but he holds up his hand and chuckles as he starts tying off loose ropes and clearing the deck. Old habits built up over a lifetime on the waves.

"I can help you sail where you will, but this weak heart of mine didn't take too kindly to those ice ghosts."

You see that he's in great pain.

"What were they, anyway, those things?"

It's a question you don't quite know the answer to, but you think of the alchemist's prophecy, the invasion and the flame. Surely all this is tied together.

Heston looks at you shrewdly, one hand on the rigging.

"The hull wasn't breached, Cap'n, and I've checked the hold. So, what's our course?"

If you want to change course and follow the ship with Casper and the crew on board, turn to **423**.

If you decide to sail straight for the Lonely Isle, turn to **183**.

301

Four pairs of sad eyes look up. Captain Hamshanks, Betty Bottle, Hairy Jonas and Shiverin' Shaun.

"Where's Casper?" you ask.

"He's got an appointment with the Dial," replies the guard, as he chains you to the wall. "And you're next."

True enough, it's not long before you're taken to a vast cavern and strapped to a post. It tilts you forwards, and a beam of light appears, casting your shadow onto some kind of metal disc. It's inscribed with rings of strange markings that start to glow and rotate. From the far side of the chamber, you hear that familiar, festering laugh. Something flashes across the disc, and darkness descends. Your adventure is over.

302

You wince as the lid creaks on its nails, and stick an arm through the opening. At first you think the crate must be empty, then you touch something cold. So cold it feels like you've plunged your hand into an icy pool. With a hiss you pull out your arm and leap from the cart. It's a shadow wraith! You watch as it flows from the crate and onto the road in front of you.

SHADOW WRAITH

Rounds: 4   Damage: 4

YOU

Leather armour doesn't work against shadow wraiths, so you can't use a defence bonus in this fight.

If you win, turn to **418**.

If you lose, turn to **261**.

303

Reluctantly, you hand over Flynt and your satchel. The pirate laughs and tosses them to one side.

"Are you out to make me a common thief, child? An old seadog fights for his loot. A pity you've got nothing to fight with but your bare hands!"

He draws his cutlass. You have no choice but to fight.

Turn to **86**.

304

You take out the book and she holds it between long thumb and forefinger.

"How does this prove her name? Has she signed it?"

You admit she hasn't, but start to tell her about the message that goes with it. The alchemist stops you.

"Anyone could write a message. That proves nothing."

You sigh and take out the locket.

Deduct 1 ABILITY point, then turn to **110**.

305

Safely below deck, Casper relaxes and smiles, and for the first time he looks his age – only a couple of years older than you.

"What are you doing here?" he asks.

And so you tell him everything that's happened since you were first woken in the night by hooded strangers. He listens with growing astonishment, and when you've finished he blows out his cheeks and laughs.

"And there was me thinking you'd just come to see your old mate, Casper!"

You grin and ask him how things are going in Port Darktide.

"Me or the town? Well, the answer's the same."

He tells you about his life since leaving Helmsgard three years ago. His father was a fisherman, and they moved here so he could join the fishing fleet.

"My mum's not been the same since he disappeared," he says. "They took him over a year back. He was one of the first. Now more people are disappearing every day. A couple were just ambushed – that's why I called out."

He shrugs his shoulders when you ask what happens to the people they take. For a moment he's lost in thought. Then he looks up.

"I know where they're from, though, the kidnappers. It's a land north of here – I know the accent. But there's something strange about them. Their blank faces... their shadows... no one believes me, but they're not right. A man walks down the street and his shadow lags behind, then catches up. He scratches his chin and the shadow scratches its nose. It's like they've got a mind of their own."

There's excitement in his voice, but in the dim light his eyes are sunken and subdued. He looks tired. Where's the bundle of energy who used to get you both into so much trouble back in Helmsgard? Your eyes briefly meet, and you feel the distance that's opened up between you. He smiles sadly, then slaps his knees and stands up.

"The Lonely Isle, was it?" he asks. "Well for once luck is with us – we'll pass it on the way to the fishing grounds. Let's hope this flame of yours can help us here in Darktide."

"You mean...?"

"I do! Come and meet the captain of the ship. She's the one that can give you passage."

Turn to **64**.

306

You come to a crossroads. If you want to go:

North, turn to **333**.   South, turn to **397**.

East, turn to **9**.   West, turn to **131**.

307

The guard draws nearer as you hurriedly lever the lid from the crate. You haven't got the time to worry about the noise, but in any case the driver seems not to notice. He turns his head slightly, and you see he has no ears. Inside the crate are bows and arrows.

If you don't already have a BOW, add it to your LOG BOOK, along with 12 ARROWS. If you do, take as many arrows as you need to have 12.

Turn to **10**.

308

"We'll take care of them for you," growls Captain Hamshanks.

With her crew close behind, she steps into the cavern and draws her cutlass. A look of surprise flits across Creeval's pale face. You run across to Casper and frantically search for a way to release him from the pillar. The fighting doesn't last long, and soon the last guard is silenced.

"You are full of surprises," Creeval calls. "Your mother would be proud."

He pauses and starts to laugh.

"But I'm afraid you won't help your friend that way."

The sound of running feet approaches. Guards stream into the cavern. Guard after guard until the crew are completely surrounded. Captain Hamshanks roars in frustration. Silence falls, then Creeval speaks again. There's a new note in his voice, as if something has occurred to him.

"You have one chance. Only one. If you discover how to free your friend, he and his crewmates will be released unharmed. I give you my word. But in return, you must stay here with me."

If you accept his offer, turn to **96**.

If you don't, turn to **415**.

309

You pick up your satchel and stash a ROPE WITH HOOK and a HOODED CLOAK. Looking around, you see Joe's violin lying smashed and broken in front of the hearth. He used to say it was the only thing that got you to sleep when you were a baby. You can almost hear the sweet, sad music that somehow flows from his rough hands.

Laying it down gently, you climb up to your room. Your BOOK OF FAIRY TALES is peeking out from under an overturned chest. It was with you in the basket that was left on Joe's doorstep, and along with the locket, it's your only link to your past. After a moment's hesitation, you put it in your satchel. Add all three items to your LOG BOOK.

Outside, a cart clatters by and somehow makes the workshop feel even emptier. You wedge the door shut, and turn towards the city centre.

If you'd like to go to the market to find Madoc, turn to **55**.

If you'd like to report your attempted kidnapping to the City Guard, turn to **325**.

310

"No. It was *Him*. He learnt how to cut them loose. How to control them. They listen to me only because I serve Him... That's why I keep this."

He draws the dagger from his scabbard; its blade not metal, but dark shadow.

"In case He should turn them against me. But it's not enough. I need the Flame. If I could just bring it north, it would keep me safe."

He sits at the chessboard and starts to arrange the pieces.

"I will give you the length of this game to choose your fate. The saviour of my kingdom, or a slave in your own."

He laughs. That laugh again. It stirs something beyond memory...

"You were there, weren't you?" you say. "When He killed my mother."

Creeval blinks, and then continues to set up the pieces.

"I did not say," he replies, "that I didn't welcome Him at first. It was an alliance that had many advantages. But I fear that once Arkendale falls, I will have outlived my usefulness."

Turn to **190**.

311

With a last, desperate effort, you pull away from the hooded figures and plunge into The Tangles.

Turn to **194**.

312

You catch a flundel – a fair-sized fish with shimmering green scales and a white belly. It can be added to the pot for later.

"T-t-t'isn't a t-t-tiddler," says Shiverin' Shaun.

Turn to **52**.

313

He takes the turning you passed before – the one whose walls are made of ice. A dim blue light filters through from the sky far above, and after many twists and turns it leads to a stone chamber. You dart behind a pillar as Creeval turns with a furtive glance. Strange for such a powerful man. He reaches under his cloak and pulls out a dagger. Or, at least, that's what you thought it was. But when he slides off the scabbard, there's no blade to be seen. Only a slight darkness, a slight shadow perhaps, where the blade should be.

He grasps a small iron hatch on the back wall. It screeches and grinds as if it hasn't been opened in many years, and he raises the hilt above his head. But what could fit through a hole that size? Then you see it. A shadow. The head of a shadow. Stretching, twisting, sliding through the opening. The hilt comes down fast and you hear a mournful cry. The shadow drifts apart like smoke.

Creeval slides the hatch shut and sheaths his weapon. Then he utters a few words in a strange language and a doorway appears in the ice. He walks through and it disappears behind him. You run into the chamber and run your hands over the wall, but can find no sign of it.

If you'd like to go back to the junction and take the other path, turn to **165**.

If you'd like to look through the hatch, turn to **284**.

314

You look from the message to the page, then back to the message. But you can make nothing of it. Deduct 1 ABILITY point.

Suddenly, Madoc leans forward.

"It's about the pictures in the margins. Look! There's the rising sun. Now draw a line to the setting sun on the other side, up to the full moon, then down to the flame underground. And there – the lines make a cross over that tree with the mark on its trunk..."

He peers closely and gasps.

Turn to **254**.

His kindly old face is strained with the effort of trying to remember.

"He warned me that trouble was brewing. The innkeeper of the Cat and Coracle said the same. People disappearing from the border towns. So we set up a watch. Reports came in of a darkness advancing from the coast. People arrived at our gates, wives without husbands, children without parents."

For the briefest moment a cloud seems to pass across his face.

"And then the shadows came and our defences were useless."

He looks down at the floor.

"He saved us, you see, Rowan. He is our saviour."

"No Joe," you say in a choked voice. "He's not."

"There was no food. No help. Those of us left were hiding in hovels. And then they found me and made me see. What use is freedom, if it's only freedom to suffer?"

His mouth twists into a smile but his eyes are dead.

"He asked about you, Rowan. He honoured me with a personal visit while I was in the Black Tower."

"The Black Tower?"

"The old Astronomer's Tower. It's where they free you from your shadow. That's where we must go now."

His rough, warm hand closes over your wrist.

"Can you stand?" he asks.

You shrink away from his touch.

"We must go, Rowan."

He leans over, silhouetted against the window, but no shadow falls across your bed. You look around wildly and see your bag hanging from the hook on the wall. You twist around and grab it.

If you have HANDCUFFS and would like to use them, turn to **74**.

If not, turn to **225**.

316

The shadow surges forwards in silence, then stops suddenly in mid-air. Slowly, almost tentatively, it raises its arm. You wait. It's almost as if it's pointing at something...

You take a step back and glance down. The white flower! You'd forgotten it was even there, stuck between the coarse fibres of your tunic. Is that what it's seen – or is it just a trap to get you to lower your blade?

If you'd like to hand the WHITE FLOWER to the shadow, turn to **151**.

If you decide not to, turn to **387**.

317

Branches claw and brambles clutch, but you don't slow down until the cries have faded to nothing. Only then do you stop and look around. You're in Gloamwold Forest. This place has a sinister reputation. Mothers say to their children: "If you don't behave I'll leave you for the old lady of the woods to find – and that will be the end of you!" Even seasoned travellers won't set foot in the forest after dark. And yet here you are, lost and exhausted. You stumble on until you come across a tree standing slightly apart from the rest. Its thick trunk is knotted and gnarled, and clear water has pooled in a hollow between its roots. You're about to scoop some to your lips when you hear a quick, high-pitched voice by your side.

"I wouldn't do that if I were you... or would I?"

You look down in surprise to see an impish creature with curly red hair and pointy ears. There's a teasing smile on her lips.

You ask her what she means.

"If I were me, I know what to do... But if I were you, I don't suppose I would."

She cocks her head and shrugs.

If you want to ignore this annoying creature and quench your thirst, turn to **392**.

If you decide not to take a drink, turn to **179**.

318

You give a warning cry, and the acrobat leaps from the cart with cat-like grace. But your captor is only a fraction too late – and instead of killing the acrobat his weapon grazes your arm. You scramble from the cart and call out for help, yelling that you've been kidnapped.

Deduct 1 LIFE point and turn to **44**.

319

Its cry sinks into the chamber walls as your brother's shadow drifts apart at last. You sheath your blade.

Turn to **207**.

320

You come to a crossroads. A horrible, sucking, crunching noise comes from the middle of the chamber. You hold your lantern high, then cry out and drop it to the floor. In the darkness, the noise stops. You hear something unnatural slithering your way. Dropping to your knees, you scrabble for the lantern, and when you hold it up your horrified face stares back, reflected over and over in a cluster of moist, black eyes. The creature rears up and its thin front legs flail. You see tufts of rat fur stuck to its pincers, but the real terror is further back, where the body of a gigantic centipede merges with the body of a gigantic snake. Is this one of the alchemist's experiments that Madoc talked about? You might have glimpsed a red chain around its throat, but you can't be sure.

If you want to attack the creature, turn to **142**.

If you decide to back away slowly, turn to **209**.

You take the BOOK OF FAIRY TALES from your satchel. Its green cover is faded with age. You lay it down on the kitchen table and read out your mother's message:

> *Now turn your thoughts to tales of old,*
> *Where dragons guard the mountain's gold,*
> *And plot your path from east to west,*
> *Where the sun does rise to where it sets,*
> *Then up to the moon that's fat and round,*
> *... But your journey's end burns underground.*
> *Look once more at the route you've traced,*
> *Where two paths cross you'll meet your fate.*

You show Madoc the title of the book. It's called *Tales of Old*.

"It was wrapped inside my clothing," you say. "Old Joe found it when he took me in. A small book of fairy tales. I thought it was just something my parents used to read to me, but look, it's in the first line of the message – and only I would know what it means!"

Madoc looks at you in astonishment.

"And read the second line," you continue, turning to a page in the book that shows a dragon among snow-capped peaks. "The message must be hidden in this picture!"

Look at the picture opposite. If you follow the instructions correctly, and trace the route with your finger, a number will appear. Multiply that number by itself and turn to the resulting entry.

If you can't find the number, turn to **314**.

322

The alchemist snatches away the flask and brings a drop to her lips. Her brows knit together in disgust. Pouring the rest away, she prods you back towards the pipes while hitting you over the head with her cane.

"A child's brain on a child's shoulders – is this what we have to place our hope in?" she mutters furiously. "Look – follow my cane."

She squints as she traces out the routes for you, getting you to collect the water from the correct outlets. Then she turns abruptly and hobbles from the chamber. Despite her age, you have to hurry to keep up, and soon you're both back in the laboratory.

Deduct 1 LIFE point and 1 ABILITY point and turn to **365**.

323

There's no time left – you pick a square and leap. The beast rears and scrapes and tries to pull its great weight up before the ground disappears beneath it. But it's too late. The Sentinels lift their orbs, and each one shoots bolts of lightning in eight directions at once. The dragon's screams mingle with your own. You weren't on the safe square.

The last thing you see is a strange shadow standing over you with pale, glimmering eyes.

"You didn't listen, Rowan. Neither did she. But there's one thing I want you to know."

A face flickers through like a storm cloud lit by lightning.

"I'm your..."

But your eyes close for the last time. Your adventure ends within touching distance of the chamber of the Flame.

324

"Curse you, Rowan," Odan gasps. "I wanted to take you alive."

As you hit the deck, you find your gaze level with the frozen eyes of Heston Gurgle. The noises above fade, and a vision hovers before you. It's a small flame, flickering, guttering, then dying in a dark and empty chamber.

325

The steps to the station lead up to a pair of studded oak doors. You push them open and walk inside. A thin guard with a downturned mouth is sitting behind the desk. He purses his lips and carries on writing as you approach. Undaunted, you tell him everything that's happened, and when you mention the gang's leader the nib of his pen breaks and he looks up. He motions to someone and the doors are bolted behind you.

"What did you say your name was?" he asks.

Suddenly you notice a large red patch on the floor. Someone has tried to scrub it out. You're grabbed from behind and hit over the head. As the world goes dark you hear the man behind the desk sigh.

"Better get Mr Griblin," he says. "We've found what he's looking for."

When your eyes open you see Lester Griblin, chief of the City Guard, standing over you. His gold chain of office rests on his substantial belly.

"Looks like he's coming round," he says, in a voice that has none of its usual pomposity. It sounds almost cringing.

And then you see why. A deathly face comes into view. Its

sightless eyes stare down, somehow seeing more than yours ever could.

"You are your mother's child, Rowan. But you've caused me enough trouble. Time to sleep now."

He raises his hand, and even though you fight it with all your strength, you feel your eyelids closing once more.

Turn to **241**.

326

You drag the bodies into a dark passage, and it's only then that you recognise one of the faces. It's Owen the gatekeeper. His daughter was in your class at school, and he used to bring around a rabbit or two for Old Joe if he'd been out hunting. Sometimes he'd put his feet up by the fire, take you in his lap and tell you tales he'd made up during his long hours on watch.

Now he looks up at you with the same glassy stare as all the others, and you curse the Shadow Reaper with a choking hatred. Swearing vengeance, you walk the short distance left to Madoc's.

Turn to **379**.

327

You take aim and let fly. Roll one DICE.

If you roll 1-3, turn to **428**.

If you roll 4-6, turn to **54**.

328

All three guards rush towards you, but one of them cries out and falls to the floor, clutching his foot. The others make it through your makeshift trap, so you'll have to fight them both at once.

If you lose a round, add together the damage ratings of the two guards (not forgetting to deduct your armour bonus from them both first), then take the total from your LIFE points. If a guard is dead, don't add their damage rating. If you win a round, deduct the COMBAT points only from the guard you chose to attack. Remember to keep a note of how many rounds you have left for each guard.

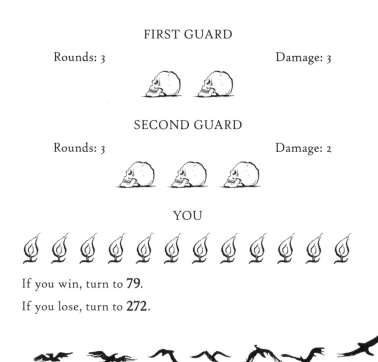

FIRST GUARD

Rounds: 3   Damage: 3

SECOND GUARD

Rounds: 3   Damage: 2

YOU

If you win, turn to **79**.

If you lose, turn to **272**.

329

Black marble statues flank the passageway. Carvings of gods or monsters, it's hard to tell. Green flames flicker and cast leaping shadows on the walls. Except, it's not always the shadows you have to look out for.

If your SIXTH SENSE level is 7 or higher, turn to **13**.

If it's 6 or lower, turn to **172**.

330

Drawing on your last reserves of strength, you make it across the deserted square. Gain 1 ABILITY point.

You see the flag of the City Guard hanging outside a large stone building. Lamps burn by the entrance. Stumbling up the steps, you bang on the doors. The feet behind you slow and you bang again. Why is no one answering? Then you turn and realise there are no guards by the steps. And the palms of your hands are sticky and wet. Holding them to the lamplight, you see they are red with blood. Your pursuers walk towards you, their faces hidden by their hoods. You hear a bolt drawn back, and the doors open. There in front of you is the leader, the one you had somehow forgotten. He's standing in the doorway, his eyes still sightless and his laugh still worse.

"We are well met, young apprentice," he says, and pauses. "You did well to get this far. I'm glad these guards did not die in vain."

There's a trail of blood leading into the room, and it ends with a pile of limp bodies. His voice hardens.

"Tie him!"

You're bound and gagged, and his laugh seems to creep from all sides as you're carried away.

Turn to **94**.

331

The traders are hawking the last of their wares as you enter the square. A rough voice rises above the din. "Don't delay, ladies and gentlemen! The shadow lengthens and winter is nearly upon us!" The trader holds up a fur coat so thick that it looks like the bear's still inside. Beside him, a clockmaker sits hunched at his stall. His inventions are spread out, and one of them tolls the hour, two miniature skeletons jerking into life to ring a silver bell. It seems to be the signal for the traders to pack up their stalls. You quicken your pace, looking for the mapmaker you were told would be here.

As you head towards the far side of the market, the stalls become shabbier and the crowds thinner. Your hand moves to the silver bracelet. What was it for? You look down and let out a quiet gasp. The green stone is glowing. You clasp your hand to your wrist, and then you see something out of the corner of your eye. A stall you hadn't noticed before, covered in shabby drapes. Inside, something glows. Something glows *green*. You duck under the drapes and find a man with bright grey eyes and grey hair. He holds up his wrist and you see a bracelet like yours. You look around and see maps rolled and maps spread.

"They're looking for you," he says in a low voice, and points across the square.

A city guard is moving quickly through the crowd.

"We must go."

He rolls up the maps and loads them into a pack that he slings across his back. Together, you leave the square.

Turn to **355**.

332

The goblin is so nimble and small that it's like trying to swat away a fly. By the time you fall face down in the mud, you're bleeding from a dozen different places at once. Your skull will be too large to hang from her belt – but perhaps she'll use it to decorate her hut.

333

You come to a crossroads. If you want to go:

North, turn to **306**.   South, turn to **57**.

East, turn to **248**.   West, turn to **131**.

334

Gripping Flynt in one hand and the shadow blade in the other, you advance to meet your brother. It's a difficult way to fight, but you have the skill to do it, and it means you can be sure of striking either his body or his shadow after a successful roll.

SHADOW REAPER

Rounds: 8   Damage: 4

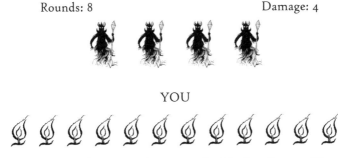

YOU

Leather armour doesn't work against the Shadow Reaper. You can only use a defence bonus if you have a CHAINMAIL VEST. Also, if he still has his staff, whenever you roll a double you're hit by a purple bolt, and must deduct 1 LIFE point regardless of whether you win or lose the round.

If you win, turn to **19**.

If you lose, turn to **391**.

335

You're woken from a deep sleep by a sharp tug on your leg. The tip of Flynt is already pressed against the ribs of a thin, shadowy figure bent over your satchel. The speed of your reaction surprises even you.

"Careful there, young warrior with the quick arm. Can't an old man be allowed to stumble in the dark? By all that's sharp and cold, Lowthorn means you no harm!"

He draws himself up and hits his bald head against the oil lamp.

"Oh, ow! We meet again!" he exclaims, shaking his fist at the swinging lamp.

"I am built for finer rooms with higher ceilings," he sighs, lovingly running his hands over a tatty fur collar.

"But times are hard for us all, or else why would one so young be travelling alone? Come, let me buy you breakfast before you go on your way."

You steal a glance around the room and see that you're attracting unwelcome attention from some of the other hammocks. You look from them to the spindly old man with the shiny head and ratty moustache.

If you'd like to accept his offer, turn to **106**.

If you'd prefer to leave the hostel at once, turn to **210**.

336

Fear creeps onto Creeval's face. His eyes widen. Eyes that seem blind yet miss nothing.

"Look at it there, on the wall."

He points at your shadow.

"That is a being of pure impulse. Every wild thought you've ever had, every flash of anger or moment of inspiration comes from your shadow... And while it's tethered to your body you have it under control, but if it were cut loose – what then?"

He stares at you intently.

"The body still lives but the spirit is gone. No individuality, no rebellion – the perfect slave. And the shadow? The shadow lives too. Beyond thought, beyond reason. A demon of pure energy."

His hand strays to the hilt of his dagger.

"You think I created the Dial?"

If 'yes', turn to **37**.

If 'no', turn to **310**.

337

There's a new system in place on the main street. People are walking in one direction on your side, and the opposite direction on the other. The centre of the street is divided for horses and carts in the same way. Fortunately, the side you need is in the shade, so you keep your head down and join the procession. No one shouts and no one swerves out of line. People talk calmly, quietly. A bead of sweat trickles down your forehead and you wipe it away. Maybe it's the backstreet kid in you, maybe it's the fear of being caught, but all you want to do is run and get to Madoc's as quickly as possible.

If your SIXTH SENSE level is 7 or higher, turn to **243**.

If it's 6 or lower, turn to **199**.

338

You dart through a doorway and find yourself in a shop filled with old books and bottles. Dust swirls inside a shaft of light coming from a window high on the back wall. An ancient shopkeeper sits behind the counter. His head has fallen forwards onto his chest, and he's wheezing in his sleep. You keep to the shadows, and wait. A few moments later, someone enters. It's Woad Griblin, loathsome son of Lester Griblin – chief of the City Guard! The two of you have never got on. In fact, he doesn't like anyone from the Craftsmen's Quarter. More than once he's taunted you for building the bed that he sleeps on.

But what's he doing following you down this quiet street? You decide to find out. Woad leaps back when you step from behind the bookcase, but he recovers quickly and pulls a pair of strange-looking weapons from his belt. Each one is the size of a hammer, with a head like a pickaxe. He weaves them through the air in a complex pattern, and you ask if he learnt that from his expensive tutor. He snarls.

"You think you're clever, 'prentice rat? You've no idea what's going on. But soon you will!"

WOAD GRIBLIN

Rounds: 4   Damage: 2

YOU

Unknown to you, each war hammer is coated in poison. If Woad wins four rounds, deduct the damage and go straight to the defeat entry.

If you win, turn to **153**.

If you lose, turn to **182**.

339

You're about to launch into your story when Casper interrupts.

"His reasons are his." He elbows you in the ribs. "My friend is asking for safe passage, and I said there's no ship safer."

Her green eyes narrow. Then she breaks into a gold-toothed grin.

"He's right, you know," she says, clapping Casper on the shoulder.

Deduct 1 ABILITY point, then turn to **161**.

You don't know what Madoc looks like, but you were told to wear the silver bracelet with the green stone when you went to meet him. You pull back the sleeve of your tunic and let out a quiet gasp. The stone is glowing. You look up and see a man striding over from the far side of the square. As he draws near he holds up his wrist and you catch the same green glow. His eyes are bright grey. They almost look too young for a face that's lined by age.

"Come with me," he says. "Quickly."

Turn to **355**.

341

The fall wakes you, slipping from Wowl's back as he lands.

"Get up!" the alchemist cries, poking you with her staff. You see a crescent moon shining through tall trees, and she leads you along a narrow path to the edge of the forest. Below, the black sea stretches to meet a sky that's bright with stars. She points towards a small town huddled on the shore.

"That is Port Darktide, on the western shores of Arkendale. From there you can charter a ship to the Lonely Isle. It's said that in ancient times there was a great stretch of land with a gleaming city surrounded by wheat fields and orchards. One day the earth awoke and the land sank beneath the waves. All was lost save for one small island, jutting like a gravestone from the sea. Maybe that is the place that 'no longer exists'."

She sighs.

"In any case, it's our best hope."

You ask if she can take you there, but she shakes her head.

"Wowl would draw too much attention. And Rowan, I am an old woman whose power lies in her books. I would be no use to you."

She raps you on the head, but gently this time.

"Go. You might be stronger than you know."

If you'd like to head straight down the slope towards the town, turn to **177**.

If you'd prefer to keep to the trees and follow the forest as it curves down the slope to the left, turn to **258**.

If you decide to scramble down a steep slope to the right, and follow a river heading towards the town, turn to **73**.

342

"Those were my orders."

You ask who gave them.

"The Shadow Reaper."

Your eyes narrow, and you ask if that was who woke you in the night.

He shakes his head, and further questions about the Shadow Reaper all yield the same response:

"That is not for me to know."

You hang your head in frustration at the man's strange, almost mechanical replies, and ask if he knows where he's taking you, at least.

"To Floriven Bridge, where we'll meet the others."

You know that bridge. It's only a couple of leagues from the city walls. If you're going to try to escape, you haven't got much time.

If you want to ask another question, turn to **111**.

If you decide you've heard enough, turn to **12**.

343

Creeval sneers.

"What a shame. I thought you might be of use to me, Idriel's child. But she would never have entrusted the secret to such a fool. Now, witness your fate."

His head tilts back and he intones in a strange language.

Turn to **411**.

344

Aware of the time ticking away, you run down back ways and side streets until finally you turn onto your old road. When you see the workshop you stop dead. The door hangs on its hinges and a window has been smashed. Inside, the place has been ransacked. Your old crib stands upended, over in the corner by Joe's bed. You pick it up and set it back on its rockers.

There's no sign of Old Joe.

If you have a CITY GUARD'S BADGE, turn to **309**.

If you don't, turn to **174**.

345

You grab hold of the tailgate and climb up without a sound.

Turn to **256**.

346

The "arm" you're clinging to bends beneath your weight until you're face to face with the lifeless lure. With the last of your strength you reach down and pull the firecrackers from your satchel. As the arm slips from your grasp, you hurl them into the pit and plunge into the creature's gullet. The firecrackers light up a pink, glistening throat, and a pool of frothing liquid below. You land with a splash. Almost at once you feel your skin burning – the creature's stomach juices are starting their work! You cry out in the gurgling darkness. But then you feel a shudder, and the whole pit convulses as a great force erupts beneath your feet. You find yourself shooting back towards the clear night sky – your firecrackers have upset the creature's stomach and sent the contents spewing upwards! The partially decomposed head of a deer rides beside you at the crest of the torrent. You're ejected from the creature's mouth and land back near the path, covered in slime and shaking from your narrow escape.

On the ground next to you, also thick with slime, you see a silver ring carved in the shape of a shield. You shudder and wonder how long it had lain in that foul creature's stomach. After washing both yourself and the ring in a nearby stream, you continue on your way.

Add a SILVER RING and delete the FIRECRACKERS from your LOG BOOK, gain 1 ABILITY point, deduct 1 LIFE point, then turn to **157**.

347

Roll one DICE.

If you roll a 2 or higher, turn to **291**.

If you roll a 1, turn to **141**.

348

Night has fallen when you find the grating with the sawn bar. You wriggle through and make your way along the alley. Buildings loom on either side, but after a few false turns you reach a road leading down to The Tangles. You whistle quietly to stop yourself from thinking about all that's happened, until a harsh shout stops the tune in your throat. A hooded figure stands at the top of the road. You take off and don't slow down until the dark streets of The Tangles close around you. Your kidnappers must have gambled on your return and gone back to Helmsgard.

You force your exhausted mind to focus. The Cat and Coracle can't be far away. The trouble is, you've only been there once before, and that was a long time ago. But at least you entered The Tangles along this same street – that will give you a chance of finding the inn, using your vague memories of the route...

Turn to **47**.

349

With your opponent off balance, you hook his ankles and give him a shove. His head strikes the ground hard, and as he tries to get up, his legs give way beneath him. But your attention is caught by movement further up the street. Three of his companions are sprinting in your direction! You turn towards The Tangles and run. With the last of your strength you fly down the hill, and the dark streets close around you.

Turn to **194**.

Suddenly you see it – bringing the gates together will form the picture of a keyhole! Maybe you need to *close* the gates to open the doors? There's only one way to find out. Slowly, with your feet scrabbling on the icy dock, you grab the wheel to the left of the gate and start turning. The action is heavy but smooth, and as the gates connect, the outline of the keyhole pulses bright green. Then they slide back and the great stone doors swing inwards. You slip into the empty corridor beyond.

Gain 1 ABILITY point and turn to **250**.

351

You step out in front of the horses and the guards advance. The clash rings loud in the street, but no one comes to your aid. Finally, a man and a woman detach themselves from the crowd and draw concealed weapons from their cloaks. You shout out in relief... But why are they circling round behind you? And why are they closing in? Then you realise the truth. These are the secret police of New Helmsgard, and in this city of drones you'll find no help.

The innkeeper shakes the bars of the cage as you're overpowered and clamped in chains.

"I'm sorry," you say, as they shove you into the cage.

The innkeeper smiles sadly. There's so much to talk about, but you make the journey to the Black Tower in silence. Your quest ends there.

352

One of the strong men lifts the driver by the neck.

"I think this gentleman needs to lighten up," says the ringmaster. "Don't you?"

The strong man grunts and tosses him through the air. He's pounced on by a troop of clowns and one of them pulls off his boots and tickles his feet with a long, yellow nail. An acrobat somersaults into your cart and looks at you curiously.

"What have we here?" she asks. "Why are you tied up, child?"

Behind her, half-Harlan reaches for his weapon.

If you decide to warn her, turn to **318**.

If you conclude it's too much of a risk, turn to **50**.

353

You kick your feet against the boards and strain to make yourself heard through your gag. But your moans are cut short as your captor makes good on his promise. The last words you hear are Owen's, asking if the driver heard a strange noise. You'll never know whether he finds out what it was – your adventure is over before it's really begun.

354

Just as you reach the junction, you hear footsteps approaching. You dart down the passage that leads back to the entrance – and only just in time. Peering out, you see a tall man heading for the icy tunnel. That lank hair... those white eyes and pale skin – it's him! He calls over his shoulder to someone you cannot see.

"Have the prisoner made ready. We'll begin shortly."

"Yes, Lord Creeval."

So that's his name. Creeval. You have no wish to meet him in that small chamber with the hatch, so you take the other turning and see the guard disappearing down a side passage.

If you'd like to follow him, turn to **91**.

If you'd prefer to continue along the main passage, turn to **329**.

355

Madoc leads you to an old cottage on the edge of town. It stands a little apart from the newer houses that have been built nearby, and its thatched roof looks out of place next to their slate tiles.

"This used to be a woodsman's cottage," he says, bolting the door and lighting a lamp.

Night has fallen, and moonlight shines off the wet cobbles outside. He closes the curtains and hangs up his cloak. On the way to the cottage, you told him all that's happened, and now he's strangely quiet. He pulls two seats in front of the kitchen range and stokes the fire. Only when you have a steaming bowl of stew, and your boots are drying on the hearth, does he sigh and break his silence.

Add 1 LIFE point, then turn to **416**.

356

Your net snares all but one of the marsh goblins. You slow down, and turn to see that the remaining goblin has slowed too. A thoughtful look has come over his face. You stop. The goblin stops too. He licks his lips and looks up at you nervously.

If you have a bow and one or more arrows, turn to **112**.

If you do not, turn to **65**.

357

You cry out for help.

"It's not me you need to ask, my sweet."

"Then who?!"

"Whose water did you take?"

Gasping for breath, you ask her what she means.

The imp rolls her eyes. "Where did you *find* it?"

The roots tighten ominously and you point frantically at the base of the tree.

"Argh! Between the roots!"

"So..."

You gasp an apology through blue lips, and the leaves stop their hissing. Slowly, the roots uncoil and you drop to the ground.

"Old Man Tree accepts your apology!" the imp chuckles as she helps you up.

"He saves that water for the birds and beasts of the forest. Not outsiders like you. Come to mention it, what *are* you doing this deep in the forest, all alone?"

Deduct 1 LIFE point and turn to **20**.

358

You see the remains of the crew backed up against the helm of the ship. Captain Hamshanks, Betty Bottle, Hairy Jonas, Shiverin' Shaun... and Casper.

A man has appeared on deck. He has his back to you, but you've seen that lank, white hair before. He intones in a soft and powerful voice:

"You have seen what the shadows can do. What is the use in fighting a foe you cannot touch?"

The sailors shake their weapons in defiance.

"Lay down your arms and I promise you will not die. Prisoners, yes. But you will not die."

Only the captain has remained quiet. Slowly, the crew fall silent and turn towards her. Her face is white with rage. You can see muscles twitching beneath her jaw. But finally, painfully, she gives a single nod. The crew stare at her in disbelief.

"What's that, cap'n?" asks Jonas. "You want us to surrender?"

Her voice is weary, but firm.

"Don't give them your life until you can make them pay for it."

Casper looks at her long and hard, then lays down his cutlass. He kicks it onto the deck below and it stops just short of the man with the white hair, spinning round and round before coming to rest. Slowly, the rest of the crew follow his lead.

"Now, down on your knees," the man commands.

He turns to the bruised sky and begins an incantation. Lightning flashes. His eyes are white and blind. His skin deathly pale. It's the man who knocked on your door, what seems like a lifetime ago. The shadows step forward and reach out.

Casper looks down the ship one last time, and his eyes widen as he sees you peering through the hatch. His expression doesn't change, but there's the smallest flicker of a smile. An almost imperceptible nod. Then the shadow's hands close over his temples and his head jerks back in pain.

You clamp your teeth against the deck to stop yourself from crying out.

The crew slump to the floor and you hear that horrible, festering laugh. The rowers carry them onto the galley, and throw Stumpy and Cork-eared Karl overboard.

Finally, the pale man crosses the gangplank, with his long shadow trailing behind. The storm clouds clear, and your ship is left adrift and alone.

Turn to **300**.

359

You stick the crowbar under the lid and push down. The wood groans. Suddenly, the cart heaves and dips as it goes over a bump and there's a loud splintering as the lid breaks apart. You duck, certain you must have been seen, but the cart carries on at the same steady pace. The noise must have been masked by the clattering of the wheels. Peering inside the crate, you see chainmail vests. You lift one out and find it's almost as light as the leather armour you're already wearing. It gleams with a strange, dark sheen.

Delete the LEATHER ARMOUR from your LOG BOOK and replace it with the CHAINMAIL VEST. The vest gives some protection against shadow wraiths, so make a note that it decreases **any** opponent's DAMAGE RATING by 1 LIFE point.

You're about to move on to the next crate when you see a guard walking along the road.

If you'd like to try to open another crate, turn to **280**.

If you'd like to leap down from the cart to avoid the guard, turn to **187**.

360

Restore your LIFE points back to 12.

For a moment, you think that you've dreamt it – the kidnappers, the Flame, the Shadow Reaper. A soft summer's sun shines through the window and you hear the familiar clatter of tools and creak of the ladder. Old Joe's grey hair appears above the boards.

"Joe!"

He clambers up and strides across to your bedside.

"Rowan, you're awake."

You fling your arms around his neck.

"She did it!" you cry.

He looks at you in puzzlement, and then you notice something odd about his expression. There's a dullness there.

"You look tired," you say, drawing back.

"Tired? No, I don't feel tired."

The dullness is echoed in his voice.

"And who are you talking about? You've been gone for over a year, Rowan, and then I find you asleep in your bed."

The whole room seems to recede from your vision, as if you've put your eye to the wrong end of a telescope. A year?

"I thought you'd been kidnapped," he's saying.

"I was, Joe. They tried to. When you went to see your brother."

"Yes... Yes, I did go, didn't I? But that was a long time ago, and he wasn't ill."

His slow, calm voice seems to freeze the blood in your veins. It's the same tone you've heard too many times before.

"That's when you went missing. I couldn't get the guards to listen, but someone came to see me one night. A tall man I'd seen at the market. He said you'd gone on a journey."

If you want to ask if he means Madoc, turn to **414**.

If you decide to keep quiet, turn to **315**.

361

You run for the slope you scrambled down before. The river churns and icy tentacles of water reach to grab you. One of them has a woman's face at its tip, twisted with rage.

"Come back, child. Give me what is miiine."

Somehow you make the slope and scramble up. Her voice fades as you head back the way you came.

If you'd like to go straight down the slope towards Port Darktide, turn to **177**.

If you'd prefer to follow the forest down the slope to the left, turn to **258**.

362

For a brief moment the hook appears to catch on something, but it's not enough to stop your fall. With a despairing cry you plunge into the foul, damp darkness.

Delete the ROPE WITH HOOK from your LOG BOOK, then turn to **197**.

363

Your hands enter the shadow, and you feel a sudden burning under the silver ring you forgot you were wearing. The shadow hisses and some kind of smoke fills your nostrils. Then it's gone, leaving a fierce cry that hangs in the air. The ring glows with a white light.

Without realising it, you've picked up a ring that protects its wearer from dark magic. But you see its power is limited. The attack has left the ring tarnished and noticeably thinner than before – it will only be able to save you from one more shadow wraith. You also find that because you've suffered no injury, your strength quickly returns. But your relief is short-lived – another shadow is gliding towards you.

Turn to **291**.

364

Your instincts tell you to be careful. Peering up the street, you see a dark figure standing against the moon. One of your pursuers is stationed between you and the town square! There's no way to make it across the street without being seen, and you can't just wait for them to search the stables. The only option left is to make a run for The Tangles. But can you outrun a full-grown man? As you weigh the odds, one of the horses behind you stamps its feet in the cold night air. A smile creeps across your face.

Turn to **140**.

365

The alchemist leafs rapidly through the book she showed you before, then looks up.

"Give me your hand."

Before you can reply you feel a sharp pain in your finger. She squeezes a drop of blood into the flask.

"Sit there," she says, pointing to a spot by the wall where there's no chair.

The charcoal burners are stoked, and potions are carefully taken down from the shelves. As she sets to work, flashes of light throw long shadows on the wall. Her hands move so quickly you can hardly follow what they're doing, and your thoughts wander back over all you've been told. Suddenly you feel a familiar rap on the head.

"Get up!" she cries. "The Flame burns low, or have you forgotten already?"

If you have a RED CHAIN in your LOG BOOK, turn to **268**.

If not, turn to **119**.

366

Creeval's white eyes follow you across the cavern and up the stone steps. From the ledge you have a better view of the contraption Casper is fixed to. It looks like a giant sundial. His shadow falls across three rings of symbols. You remember seeing those rings rotate around the dial, just before the light came on.

Creeval hands you the open book, and says in a voice that's as cold and smooth as a snake's skin:

"So, Rowan. How many spaces clockwise shall I move each ring? Tell me the inner one first, and work your way outwards." He smiles. "There are no tricks."

Turn the page to see the book and the dial itself. Use both to work out how to free Casper, by turning to the number that you must give to Creeval.

If you can't work out the number, turn to **343**.

Your reckless actions can't help but draw attention in this city of drones. People turn to stare as you run out into the middle of the street, and up ahead two figures detach themselves from the crowd. You turn to see you're being followed by two more. These are the secret police of New Helmsgard. You dodge into an alley and your footsteps echo loudly. It's not long before they're joined by many more. The way back is cut off. You splash through puddles that rarely see the light of day, and come to a skidding halt. Up ahead is a brick wall. It's a dead end.

After a fierce but brief struggle, you're overpowered and transported to the Black Tower for processing. Your quest ends there.

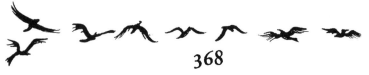

368

For every round you lose, roll one DICE before deducting your LIFE points. If you roll an even number, Pustula injects venom with his bite, and you must double the damage rating before deducting your armour bonus.

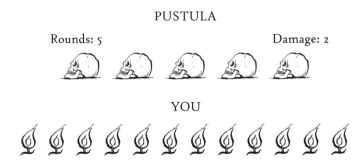

PUSTULA

Rounds: 5   Damage: 2

YOU

If you win, turn to **211**.

If you lose, turn to **132**.

369

A young guard tackles you to the floor.

"Save the child!" Madoc shouts.

The big butcher tips over the table with a roar, sending flagons scattering in all directions. But the rest of the guards have not been slow to react. It's hard to see exactly what's going on, with your head pressed into the gritty floor, but you hear the clash of weapons.

"Weedle, you know the orders," someone shouts.

"Dead or alive," the guard on top of you whispers.

You see Madoc fighting desperately to reach you, but it's too late. The noise fades and the room goes dark. Your adventure is over.

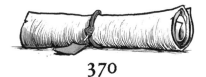

370

Your feet may as well belong to a tailor's dummy. They're so numb that you have to rely on sight alone as you lower them carefully from foothold to foothold. Somehow you make it most of the way down before your eyes are deceived. A snow-covered ledge turns out to be snow all the way through, and you find yourself dangling by your fingertips. You look down. It's not too far. If you get a bit of luck with the landing...

Roll one DICE.

If you roll a 1, 3 or 5, turn to **206**.

If you roll a 2, 4 or 6, turn to **133**.

Gain 1 ABILITY point.

"The keys are on his belt," whispers the Captain.

As you approach the cell, you see the dark outlines of your old crew. The door screeches on its hinges, and you release them from their chains. They're half-frozen with cold.

"I can hardly move my fingers," complains Hairy Jonas, shaking his hands up and down. "More like flippers."

"T-t-t'ain't warm!" says Shiverin' Shaun.

You ask where Casper is, although you already know the answer.

"They took him away, just before you got here," says the Captain.

"The guard said something about a dial," Betty Bottle adds. "Strapping him to a dial."

"We'll see about that," growls the Captain.

She strides across to a small guard's room and comes back with the crew's old weapons.

"Ready?" she asks.

Cutlasses rattle in response.

"Aye," says Hairy Jonas. "We're ready."

As they prepare to leave, you check the other cells, but they're all empty. What happened to the people inside?

Turn to **84**.

372

A shadow appears from nowhere. You dodge into a side street, but it slides straight for you.

SHADOW WRAITH

Rounds: 4   Damage: 4

YOU

Leather armour doesn't work against shadow wraiths. You can only use a defence bonus if you have a CHAINMAIL VEST.

If you win, you can turn back to the **previous entry** to continue your quest.

If you lose, turn to **261**.

373

Your vision starts to blur, but somehow you force your legs to keep moving. You are almost across the square when your foot catches on a cobblestone and your pursuers are upon you. In no time you're bound and gagged.

As a sack is pulled over your head, the last thing you see is the lamps of the City Guard station, burning brightly on the far side of the square.

Turn to **94**.

374

You turn and stagger a few paces down the street towards the old docks. After all you've been through you can't quite believe this is the end. But it is. You sink to the ground. The Shadow Reaper has won.

375

The second rat squeals past your ear, its big yellow teeth gnashing at thin air. You dash through the door and onto the street. It's only when you get to the crossroads that you slow down and consider where you are. After a few moments to catch your breath, you set off for the docks.

Turn to **78**.

376

The passage leads down to a small chamber. It feels much older than the rest of the citadel. Tree roots push through the walls, and the room is bare except for a shallow basin made of green stone.

"Let's have a look at you, Rowan."

A dark form stands between you and the basin. It looks like a shadow, but has pale, glimmering eyes and a staff that flickers with purple flame. There's something else, too...

"I can talk, yes. We're both here, Rowan. My shadow... and me."

He laughs, and a face flickers through the darkness like a cloud lit by lightning. A young face.

"Do you see me? Do you see your poor, forgotten brother?"

The face flashes into view once more, his mouth twisted into a grin, hatred in his eyes.

"They didn't tell you about the rejected one, did they? About the older brother who wasn't good enough."

The flames on the staff flare and coil.

"Well here he is. And hasn't he been busy? The whole of Arkendale bent at the knee, the old magic gone."

He points his staff.

"If I can't have it, no one can."

A purple bolt strikes your satchel and it bursts into flames. You drop to the floor and smother them with your tunic. Deduct 1 LIFE point.

Your brother laughs.

"Rowan, you weren't even born when your mother told me I could never be the Guardian. I bear you no malice. Why do you think I sent kidnappers, not assassins?"

Again the face flickers through, and the grin has gone.

"I am alone."

You stare in silence.

"What have you done to yourself?" you ask eventually.

"I made myself strong. How else do you think I could control them? The shadows. But Rowan, my mind is the same. I'm your brother. Why not join me? You could stay as you are, and together we would rule Arkendale."

You look deep into his pale eyes. The request is genuine. It takes you by surprise. Perhaps, at the end of your long journey, there's another way. Perhaps he would listen to you...

If you accept his offer, turn to **68**.

If you reject it, turn to **267**.

377

The streets are thick with people either scurrying to the market or trudging back. You'd forgotten how busy it gets on market day. Roll one DICE.

If you roll 1-2, turn to **344**.

If you roll 3-4, turn to **282**.

If you roll 5-6, turn to **87**.

378

You fought bravely, but the guard overpowers you in the end. With sweat dripping from his brow, he binds your wrists and marches you from the square.

"Don't see what they want with such a scrawny little runt anyway," he mutters, giving you a rough shove as you head towards the station.

Turn to **325**.

379

The windows of Madoc's cottage are blind with dust – it's clear that no one's lived there in a long time. To your surprise the door swings open with a gentle push. Your feet crunch on dead leaves, and you see that Madoc's cloak and boots are gone. A grim smile spreads across your face. So, he got out then.

You sit down to rest your feet for a moment. Your eyes fall on the leaves around the door, and you realise someone must have been coming in and out. Your hand hangs down and touches something warm and soft...

"Boska!" you cry.

Madoc's old cat mews and rubs himself against your legs.

"So it was you!"

The old tom stretches and yawns. Then he saunters across to a loose floorboard by the hearth and starts to scratch.

"They're not after your shadow, are they, puss?" you say, resting your head against the back of the chair.

"I don't think it would work on you anyway. Cats are all shadow... What are you doing, Boska?"

He's still scratching at the floorboard, but with a determination that makes you sit up. You see it's loose at one end. Grabbing the poker by the hearth, you lever it up. The old board creaks and something underneath catches your eye. It's a small leather pouch. Carefully, you tip a gold ring into your palm. In the dim light, you see it's inscribed with ancient runes. A shiver runs down your spine as you slide it on. You feel somehow sharper, more alert.

There's a short message, written on a scrap of paper. 'Keep the ring safe until the Guardian emerges.'

Boska licks his paw and looks very pleased with himself. You scratch him behind the ears.

"Did he wonder whether I was the Guardian, Boska? Whether all our hopes rested on me?"

Before you leave, you wash and dress your wounds, and make a hasty meal of dried meat and blackberry cordial. Then you set off for your last remaining hope: the alchemist's laboratory.

Add the GOLD RING to your LOG BOOK, and make a note that in combat it increases your dice roll by 1 against all opponents. For example, if you roll an 8, the ring turns it into a 9.

Add 5 LIFE points, then turn to **113**.

380

"Did you notice how the hooded men never made a sound as they fought?" Madoc asks. "And their expressions never changed... I've seen that before – at your mother's hall, when it was attacked."

You tell him their leader wasn't there. The man with the pale face and strange eyes.

He nods as you reach his cottage.

"We'd better take a look at that book of yours."

Turn to **321**.

381

The 'arm' you're clinging to bends beneath your weight until you're face to face with the lifeless lure. Slowly, slowly, it slips from your grasp and you plunge into the foul, damp darkness.

Turn to **197**.

382

Soon, the river is flowing naturally once more, but who knows for how long? Your heart thumps in your chest as you splash downstream. Then, just as you're about to climb out, you notice a small point of blue light being carried on the current. You snatch it from the water. It's a stone carved with a simple design, showing a river running into the ocean. The whole stone glows with a soft blue light. With one last look along the valley, you scramble up the slope.

Add a BLUE STONE to your LOG BOOK, then turn to **157**.

383

Slowly, arms aching with the effort, you drag yourself up and into the cart.

Turn to **256**.

384

You dream you're in the town square. It's market day, and through the crowd you catch a glimpse of Old Joe. You call out, but he doesn't hear you. He's walking away, and you fight your way over and grab his arm. It's bony and thin. He turns, but it's not his face. The eyes stare down, sunken and sightless, and the mouth twists into a smile.

"All roads lead to us, Rowan. Don't you remember?"

You wake to a bang at the door. It's the innkeeper, bringing you a plate of food and a bowl of water. The sun slants in at the window. You leap up and splash some water in your face.

"It's past midday," the innkeeper says. "I let you sleep as long as

I could."

Turn to **435**.

385

The shadow reaches for your heart and you bring your hand up to your chest. There's a sudden hissing sound, and a smell like burning flesh. A long wail fills the chamber as you watch the shadow drift apart. The silver ring on your finger glows with a white light.

Make a note of the number of this entry (385). Then, if this is the first time the ring's been used, turn to **408**. If it's the second time, turn to **49**.

Then, turn to **126**.

386

You approach slowly, and all the time the figure in the shawl hauls the bucket up from the well. Round and round the wheel squeaks.

"Are you the Old Lady of the Forest?" you ask. "I was told to find you. That you could help me."

With a dull clank, the bucket reaches the top. The figure lifts it to the ground and you look for a face under the shawl, but see none. An arm extends and points to the bucket. At first, all you can see is the blue sky reflected in the water. Then clouds start to gather, even though there are none overhead. They form the face of a young girl.

"Do you think I should look my age?" the face asks, with a voice that sounds like the rustling of leaves.

You open your mouth, but the water shivers as the face turns to a skull.

"I know your story. I know more than you know. So listen to me. There's a new magic gathering on the borders of Arkendale. It threatens the old magic. It will overrun the kingdom and destroy my forest. See what awaits."

You lean closer as Helmsgard appears in the water. Prisoners are being carted through the streets. You see Old Joe's face pressed against the bars. The ramshackle Astronomer's Tower has gone, and in its place looms a tower of black stone. A huge furnace is fed by an unending stream of trees, as ancient Gloamwold is cut to stumps.

The face reappears.

"Go back to Helmsgard and find Madoc the mapmaker. It was he who left you on the carpenter's doorstep, and he who has what you need. Go to the market wearing this, and you will meet him there."

The shrouded figure hands you a silver bracelet with a green stone, then points at a path that's appeared through the trees.

Add a SILVER BRACELET to your LOG BOOK.

If you decide to take the path, turn to **237**.

If you want to ask The Old Lady of the Forest why she tried to trick you if she needs your help, turn to **155**.

387

The shadow waits a few moments longer, then flies at you so quickly you're taken by surprise.

SHADOW WRAITH

Rounds: 4   Damage: 4

YOU

Leather armour doesn't work against shadow wraiths. You can only use a defence bonus if you have a CHAINMAIL VEST.

If you win, turn to **104**.

If you lose, turn to **169**.

388

In one swift movement you stand and leap backwards out of the cart. Arching your back like a gymnast you use your hands to spring over onto your feet.

"Hey, that was pretty good!" yells one of the acrobats.

But you have no time to lose. You call out for help and yell that you've been kidnapped.

"What?" cries the ringmaster, puffing out his chest.

Turn to **44**.

389

You take aim from the shadows. The bow creaks softly. With time to line up your shot, this shouldn't be too difficult.

Roll one DICE.

If you roll a 2-6, turn to **186**.

If you roll a 1, turn to **62**.

390

"The Shadow Reaper himself," Pustula replies proudly.

You hear a growl behind you.

"Is that who kidnapped my crew?" Heston yells.

Pustula blinks slowly.

"I very much doubt it. Perhaps you could furnish me with a description?"

"Tall creep with hair like cobwebs and white eyes."

"Ah, you mean Creeval?" Pustula cries with indignation. "We would never work for him. That poor fool's time is almost up. Once the Shadow Reaper takes Arkendale, he'll have no more use for Creeval."

You begin to ask who the Shadow Reaper is, but a roar from Gucifer drowns you out. The tentacles around the boat start to flex and twist. Pustula trembles.

"Oh dear, Gucifer grows tired of our idle chatter. He has duties to perform and it's unwise to delay him any further."

You point out that it would be very wise for you and Heston, and Pustula nods gravely.

"That is true, I am sometimes forgetful of the client's perspective. I hope that has not tarnished your opinion of our services."

He bows, and leans down to pat the sea demon's tongue.

"Well, Gucifer, we have finished the formalities."

"Wait!" you cry.

But it's no use. The tongue withdraws and two great tentacles slither across either end of the deck. With a lurch, the ship is lifted high into the air. You wrap your arms around the mast as the deck splinters and the ship is torn in two. Heston hangs from the wheel at one end. You watch as his grip fails and he falls straight down Gucifer's throat. The sea demon roars and crushes the helm to flotsam.

Then it's your turn. He lifts you over his gaping mouth, and far below, Pustula waves cheerily. You shift your position to get a better grip.

Roll one DICE and add it to your ENDURANCE and ATHLETICISM levels.

If your total is 16 or higher, turn to **289**.

If it's 15 or lower, turn to **175**.

You don't feel the strike, but you do feel the cold earth against your cheek. You stretch for your satchel, but it's just out of reach and you can't get up. Your brother stands over you, no triumph on his face.

"My name's Ash, by the way. You never asked."

"Ash," you whisper as your eyes close.

You die with his name on your lips.

392

With a look of regal disdain you turn away and scoop up a handful of cool water.

If your SIXTH SENSE level is 4 or higher, turn to **92**.

If your SIXTH SENSE level is 3, turn to **226**.

393

The winged beasts dip their wings and dive towards you.

There are twelve arrows in your quiver. You draw one and take aim at the lead creature.

... Roll one DICE.

Roll a 6: you kill it – fill in both halves of its crossbones.

Roll a 4 or 5: you wound it – fill in one half of its crossbones.

Roll a 1, 2 or 3: you miss.

If your SKILL level is 8 or higher, add 1 to each roll. For example, a 3 becomes a 4. The GOLD RING (if you have it) does not help you in this fight.

When both halves of the creatures' crossbones are filled in, they tumble from the sky. After each roll, scribble out one of your twelve arrows below.

WINGED BEAST

WINGED BEAST

WINGED BEAST

If you kill all three creatures before running out of ARROWS, make a note in your LOG BOOK of how many you have left, then turn to **139**.

If you run out of arrows, make a note of how many of the winged beasts are still alive, then turn to **38**.

394

You run as best you can along the riverbed, focussing so much on keeping your balance that you don't notice the water draining away, flowing backwards. It's only when it's almost completely dry that you turn around. Rearing above you is a creature made entirely of water. It's a writhing mass of tentacles, silver in the moonlight. On the end of one is a woman's face. It snakes down and sways in front of you.

"Ssssilly chillld. Do you not see? I can simply take what is mine."

If you have FIRECRACKERS and would like to use them, turn to **3**.

If you have a SLEEPING POTION and would like to use it, turn to **296**.

If you have neither, or don't want to use them, turn to **101**.

395

You slip the cloak over your shoulders and pull up the hood. Your heart thuds inside your chest as you walk past the guard and into the square. Not daring to look behind, you expect to hear a shout at any moment. But none comes. With a sigh of relief you look up.

If you have the SILVER BRACELET, turn to **340**.

If you don't have the bracelet, turn to **403**.

396

The hatch catches as you try to slam it shut. You grab it with both hands, but it won't budge.

If you have a MIRROR, turn to **48**.

If you don't, turn to **269**.

397

You feel a sharp pain in your calf. You spin around in time to see a rat squeezing through a crack in the brickwork. Blood trickles down your leg. Deduct 1 LIFE point. Then you come to a crossroads. If you want to go:

North, turn to **333**.

South, turn to **57**.

East, turn to **28**.

West, turn to **320**.

398

The lady in the robe is the last to fade. She holds out her hands as you sink beneath the waves.

"Rowan, my child..."

399

You hear running water below, and enter a small chamber, almost a cave. On the back wall, a network of rusting pipes feeds a dark stream. The alchemist lights a lamp and points to the wall.

"You see at the top there, where those pipes enter the chamber? Each of those pipes carries water from one of Arkendale's eight rivers. The Wendle, the Arlas, the Merush, the Isenwell, the Endulin, the Mithensar, the Teffi and the Teer."

"Now, see how they run through a network of pipes until the water drains into the stream at the bottom? Some of those pipes are connected so that the waters from the rivers mingle. Listen carefully – to make the fuel for the Flame, I need water from four rivers: the Arlas, the Merush, the Endulin and the Teer. BUT!"

She strikes her cane into the ground for emphasis.

"The water you collect cannot be mixed with water from the Mithensar, the Isenwell, the Teffi or the Wendle."

She hands you a flask.

"My eyes aren't what they used to be. Follow the pipes. You'll need to hold this flask under more than one of those outlets to catch the four waters you need. Let's see if the Guardian's brain is bigger than their boot size."

Turn the page to see the pipes. All nine of the outlets are numbered. When you have chosen your outlets, join their numbers together, lowest first, and turn to that entry.

If you chose incorrectly, turn to **322**.

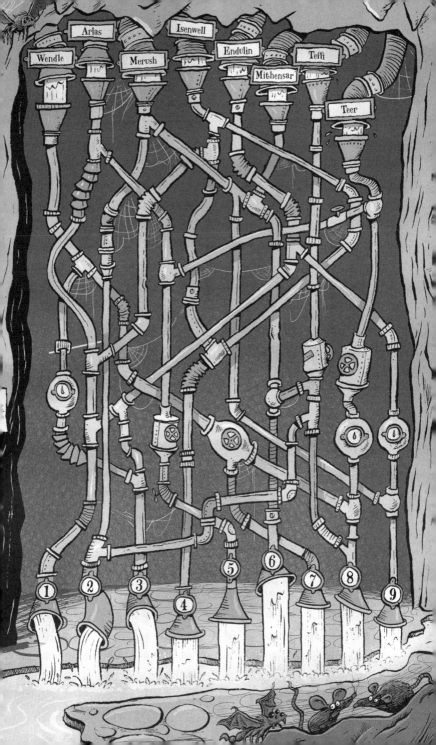

400

As you turn to leave the chamber, sparks rise from the Flame and merge into a blinding light. When you open your eyes, an image hangs in the air. You realise there are small figures moving within it. Peering closer, you see Old Joe coming out of his workshop. He scratches the back of his head and looks around. Up and down the street, doors are opening and people are stepping outside. He closes the door and there you see it: his shadow, back where it belongs. He cups his hands and shouts your name.

"I'm coming, Joe!" you cry. "I'm coming home!"

As the vision fades, you run from the chamber, back up through the shattered tower and onto the high cliffs. The sun is rising, and you see a familiar shape flying towards you. A long howl greets your wave. It's Wowl, coming to take you back to Helmsgard and Old Joe!

401

You wish the boy would step out of the shadows. But there's something in his voice that you trust, even though you remember the advice to stick to the main roads.

If you'd like to follow that advice, turn to **180**.

If you'd like to ignore the advice and enter the dark lane, turn to **97**.

402

After a quick breakfast, Madoc pushes back the table and chairs.

"I used to train young cadets," he says. "How about a few light drills before we set off?"

He puts you through a training exercise that leaves you flat on your back, fighting for breath.

Add 1 ABILITY point each to your SKILL, ATHLETICISM and ENDURANCE levels.

At the end of the session, he hands you some leather armour to wear under your tunic. Then he spreads a selection of items on the table.

"Take three," he says. "You need to travel light."

Choose **three** items from the list below. Each item can only be used when you're given the option in the text.

HANDCUFFS: bind wrists together

SLEEPING POTION: sends a person or creature to sleep

MIRROR: hand mirror with silver handle

NET: weighted at the edges to catch a moving target

FIRECRACKERS: small pouches that make a loud bang on impact

CALTROPS: spiked metal balls that can be thrown on the floor to deter pursuit

Make a note of your choices in your LOG BOOK, along with the LEATHER ARMOUR. The armour decreases an opponent's DAMAGE RATING by 1 LIFE point.

Turn to **290**.

Your heart sinks as you look around the square. You don't know what Madoc looks like, and can't attract attention to yourself by shouting his name. Anyway, there are only a few people still here. One of the last traders to leave shuffles past with a bag slung over his shoulder. You stop him and ask for help.

Turn to **242**.

404

"Odan was one of the first. He was part of a rebellion against Creeval."

Her voice lowers.

"That's when the Shadow Reaper appeared. He offered a solution – a way for Creeval to turn his people into slaves and create an army of shadows. And that was all true, but there was one thing he didn't say. One crucial thing. The shadows answer only to him! Rowan, they are beings of pure energy. Not good. Not evil. But lost, angry... unstoppable. He has found a way to control them and now Creeval is little more than a hostage in his own kingdom. And the Shadow Reaper waits... waits for the Flame to go out."

She pauses.

"Arkendale's next, Rowan. His shadow legion has little power while the Flame burns, but..."

She's fading from view and suddenly the swirling waters surround you.

"Wait," you cry. "Don't go!"

But no matter how hard you fight, the walls of the whirlpool rise.

"Please!"

"Rowan, take this."

You look down and see that you're holding the hilt of a dagger, but where the blade should be there's only a shadow.

"What is it?" you shout.

"A blade to cut shadow. And remember..." Her voice is almost lost to the whirling waters.

"... I chose you."

Add the SHADOW BLADE to your LOG BOOK, and make a note that it allows you to fight shadow wraiths, but does not increase the effect of a successful roll against them. For all other combat, use FLYNT.

Turn to **360**.

You take the flask from your satchel. The liquid inside is as dark as ever in the moonlight, and its song fills the air with a soft power. But as you tip the flask, the song takes on a sadder tone. A woman's face appears in the river. It snakes upwards to drink the liquid that you pour.

"Ahhh, yesss. And there's power in you, too. So breathe in deep, pleeease. Inhaaale."

Treacherous tentacles of icy water coil their way up until they find your mouth and nose. Slowly, your limp body is drawn down into the water. You'll never see how the riverbanks suddenly bloom with fruit trees and flowers. Nor how they wither and die as the river is poisoned by the destruction He brings, with his inevitable conquest of Arkendale!

406

You bring Flynt down hard, but miss the beast by a hair's breadth and snap the chain around its neck. You leap back, expecting it to pounce, but instead its whole body starts to shiver horribly. With a roar it collapses and writhes on the ground. Then you see the mutant has disappeared, and a great hound stands in its place. It bounds off into the dusk, as a bat flits across the moon.

Add a RED CHAIN to your LOG BOOK and turn to **348**.

407

Creeval sighs and shakes his head.

"Have you not seen my guards with no shadows? Are they not alive?"

You remind him not all of them are still alive, but he waves away your riposte.

Deduct 1 ABILITY point, and turn to **336**.

408

Without realising it, you've picked up a ring that protects its wearer from dark magic. But you see that its power is limited. The attack has left the ring tarnished and noticeably thinner than before – it will only be able to save you from one more shadow wraith.

Turn back to the **previous entry**.

409

You hold your breath as Owen chats to the driver.

"A bit early to be up and about?" he asks.

The driver laughs and says something you don't quite catch.

"Well, be careful how you go," Owen says. "There've been sightings of a group of armed men in the area. Not from around here, I've heard."

You blink back tears of frustration as the cart passes through the East gate and out of Helmsgard.

Once clear of the city, your captor sits you up and pulls away the sack. He's the only other person in the cart – the rest must be making their way out separately. His hood is drawn back, and in the weak dawn light you see a pale face with dull, grey eyes. He doesn't look that much older than you, but he stares straight ahead, seemingly uninterested in you or anything else. You make a muffled noise. After a moment's hesitation, he unties your gag and rests his hand on the hilt of his weapon. You see a name carved into it. 'Flynt.' It's not a word you've heard used around Helmsgard. You clear your throat quietly and risk a question.

In a flat voice, he tells you he's from a fishing village beyond the northern border of the kingdom. His name is half-Harlan.

Turn to **111**.

410

After regaining your breath, you decide to explore the stables. In the stalls, moonlight gleams off three pairs of dark eyes. A horse snorts and stamps. "Shhh," you whisper, and stroke its muzzle. Turning to the rest of the stable, it doesn't take long to discover that there's only one way out – and that's the way you came in. You unbar the gate and open one side.

If your SIXTH SENSE level is 4 or higher, turn to **364**.

If your SIXTH SENSE level is 3, turn to **419**.

411

The disc below Casper lights up and whirrs into life once more. The rings with their strange markings glow and rotate around the central pillar, then stop with a clunk. All is quiet. Casper's shadow is a dark, still line across the disc. He looks at you in fear and confusion. Then something flashes across the disc and all the confusion leaves his eyes forever. It's the wail you remember, not from Casper, but from his shadow, as it drifts slowly away from its body.

"Now it's your turn, carpenter's apprentice."

Creeval's laughter fills the cavern.

412

"She likes her little games, yes she does. She likes her games!" As Nettle's words echo through your mind, you look from one path to the other. Is she part of the trick, or is she here to help? As your thoughts stumble through a hall of mirrors, your eyes are free to see what's right in front of you. The path on the right, the caves in the rock face next to Nettle – they form the image of a skull! And the path on the left, with the long, trailing branches and dark cliff face, they form the image of an old lady. You've found her, hidden in plain sight.

You start down the left path and Nettle disappears. Was she ever really there? As you walk under the cliff, the ravens take off and the trees part to reveal a wide clearing, bathed in sunlight. You see a hunched figure wrapped in a shawl, drawing up water from a well.

Gain 1 ABILITY point, then turn to **386**.

413

If your SKILL level is 9 or higher, turn to **334**.

If it's 8 or lower, turn to **2**.

414

"So that's his name, is it? I asked, but he wouldn't tell me. Said a friend one day could be an enemy the next. I didn't know what he meant at the time."

Deduct 1 ABILITY point, then turn to **315**.

415

At a nod from Lord Creeval, the guards drag you away from Casper.

He calls down in a voice now dripping with scorn.

"Then watch, Rowan, and witness your fate!"

His head tilts back and he intones in a strange language.

Turn to **411**.

416

"I've been thinking about how to begin," Madoc says. "It's a long story, and I only know part of it."

The firelight deepens the lines on his face and his eyes are dark wells.

"I knew your mother. Her name was Idriel."

Your breath catches in your throat. Idriel is the name on your locket. The one Old Joe found wrapped up in your swaddling clothes when you were left on his doorstep.

"She had a great hall in the northern reaches of Arkendale, where I was captain of the guards. We often had visitors, sometimes from far outside the kingdom. They were given food and lodging, but they came to consult with your mother. I never knew what they talked about. There were books on her desk written in an ancient script."

He pauses and looks into the flames.

"One night, we were attacked. My guards were well-drilled, but their forces were strange. These men fought in silence... their expressions never changed. If one man fell, two more stepped over his body. And there were too many to hold. Your father died defending the gate."

Even in the firelight, his face looks pale.

"They forced us back until we held only the upper floor. Someone... or something called on us to surrender. That voice struck fear into my heart, but your mother didn't falter. She led me through into her chamber, where you lay, wrapped up warm for a journey. She unlocked a box and handed me a parchment. It stained red beneath her fingers, and I saw blood soaking through her chainmail. Outside, the cries were drawing near. She gave you a kiss and told me to go. As I climbed from the window with you strapped to my back, the door shuddered. She drew herself up to her full height."

Madoc looks you in the eye.

"She'd hold them off until you were safe. I knew that."

He stares right through you into the past, then his shoulders relax.

"There's not much more to say. I evaded the sentries that ringed the hall and travelled many days to a carpenter's workshop in Helmsgard, where your father said you'd be safe for a while from enemy spies."

He looks at you sadly.

"But now they've found you."

If you want to ask more about your father, turn to **115**.

If you want to ask to see the parchment, turn to **259**.

417

You make a leap for the clothesline, but it slips through your fingers and you land in a heap, jarring your ankle on the hard ground. You look around to see if anyone spotted your embarrassing attempt. Unfortunately for you, someone did – a hooded figure at the end of the alley! You run in the opposite direction, and hear that voice again, faint but mocking as it floats over the rooftops.

"All roads lead to us, little Rowan. All of them."

Deduct 1 LIFE point and turn to **42**.

418

The shadow drifts apart and is soon lost amongst the smoke that hangs over the grimy cobbles. But the cart is already disappearing up the road, and people are passing it on the way down. You turn and head for the old docks further along the river.

Turn to **187**.

419

You step onto the street, confident that you've given your pursuers the slip, but a glance around freezes you on the spot. One of the hooded figures is stationed between you and the town square! For a brief moment, you think he hasn't seen you, then his cry pierces the silence. It won't be long before his companions join him.

If you decide to stand and fight, and you have a HATCHET, turn to **154**.

If you decide to stand and fight, and don't have a HATCHET, turn to **271**.

If you choose to make a run for The Tangles, turn to **208**.

420

Your arms are almost jerked from their sockets – but the hook holds! You swing against the moist, pink sides of the creature's gullet and climb upwards before the creature can react. With your arms shaking and your breath coming in ragged gasps, you scramble onto solid ground. Below you, the creature's mouth has closed. You wonder whether it's even aware of what happened – already, the lure is back, waving and calling to you from the hollow.

After resting a while, you unhook the rope and continue on your way.

Gain 1 ABILITY point and turn to **157**.

421

She looks at you closely and nods.

"Where will you go?"

You think for a moment. Old Joe won't be back until tomorrow at the earliest, but you remember something he said a few weeks ago. You were sweeping up after work and he leant in the doorway with a strange look in his eyes.

"Get to the Cat and Coracle, Rowan. If you're ever in trouble, forget the city guards – get to the Cat and Coracle."

He wasn't a man who wasted words, so you knew that was all

you were going to get. But you saw his kindly face trying to mask his concern, and you remembered what he said.

"That's where I want to go," you say. "The Cat and Coracle inn. It's back in Helmsgard, in The Tangles."

Nettle nods.

"I'll take you as far as Toadflax Dell. It's almost a day's journey, but from there, I can show you a back way into the city."

Turn to **299**.

422

The ocean roars in your ears and the walls of the garden fade. Only the tree and the woman remain.

"Quickly Rowan," she says. "One more chance, before you sink beneath the waves."

Turn to **255**.

423

You look from the galley to the Lonely Isle, then back to the galley.

"Follow the galley," you say eventually, putting the flame from your mind. "We can't leave them."

So as the sun goes down you follow the galley's torches through a long and bitter night. At daybreak you climb down from the crow's nest for breakfast.

"We're entering the waters of the far north," Heston says.

A rasping cough overtakes him, and it's several minutes before he can continue.

"I've rarely ventured this far from the shores of Arkendale."

And still you sail on, through another night and into the next day. Despite the layers of clothing your bones ache from the cold. In the early dawn your boat rocks as a whale surfaces off the port bow. It surveys you with a great, dark eye, then disappears beneath the waves. Down below, Heston is getting quieter and quieter. If you don't make land, he won't last much longer.

Suddenly your grip tightens on the telescope. You check again. Mountains on the horizon, jagged and white. The galley drops its sails and rows into a narrow inlet.

Heston brings your ship into a sheltered cove just to the east. You drop anchor and wade ashore. There are birch trees for firewood, and the two of you share hot onion stew and coffee for breakfast.

"My pegs won't take me over that ridge, Rowan," says Heston, ladling you a second helping. "But when you find 'em, tell the Cap'n that Ol' Heston is keeping the decks swabbed."

Add 4 LIFE points, then turn to **17**.

424

Roll one DICE.

If you roll a 4 or higher, turn to **291**.

If you roll a 3 or lower, turn to **141**.

425

You try to call out for help, but your voice freezes in your throat. And besides, what help could anyone be? As your sight fades, a vision hovers in front of you. It's a small flame, flickering, guttering, then dying in a dark and empty chamber.

426

You hurriedly prise the lid from the crate. It lifts quietly, and you peer inside. The crate looks dark and empty. Then the darkness moves. With a hiss you leap from the cart. A shadow wraith! As it flows from the crate, the guard stops to watch.

SHADOW WRAITH

Rounds: 4   Damage: 4

YOU

Leather armour doesn't work against shadow wraiths. You can only use a defence bonus if you have a CHAINMAIL VEST.

If you win, turn to **239**.

If you lose, turn to **120**.

427

The old man's eyes narrow.

"You want a free lunch and a show, eh?" he says.

His voice has lost all its oiliness.

"Didn't you know, child? Nothing is free in this world. So come, my beauties, let us fight! For justice, honour and fresh cheese!"

Two rats give a determined squeak and somersault into his hands. Before you realise what's happening he has launched them at your face, and two more rats are already rolling into place, ready to be fired in the next volley.

For each rat, roll one DICE and add it to your ATHLETICISM level. If your total is 9 or higher, you manage to dodge, but if your total is 8 or lower, the rat sinks its teeth and claws into your flesh, and you must deduct 1 LIFE point.

If you managed to dodge both rats, turn to **375**.

If one or both rats bit you, they slow you down long enough for the old man to launch another two rats, and you must roll again for each of these. The thrown rats scuttle back around to the old man, so he has a continuous supply of ammunition.

428

Your arrow flies past the marsh goblin's ear. With a squeal he disappears into the long grass, and his angry chatter grows fainter and fainter.

Deduct one ARROW from your LOG BOOK, then turn to **157**.

429

The buildings get smaller as you near Madoc's cottage. In a dusty square a queue of people wait their turn at the well. There's an old scaffold, and a tattered poster pinned to the post. It's the words that stop you. 'WANTED DEAD OR ALIVE FOR THE MURDER

OF WOAD GRIBLIN.' Then you see the face underneath. Your face. Out of the corner of your eye, you see someone pointing in your direction.

Your head spins as you hurry into a quiet lane. You hadn't had a choice, had you? But your thoughts are interrupted by a guard up ahead, and you turn to see another blocking your escape. You'll have to fight them both at once.

If you lose a round, add together the damage ratings of the two guards (not forgetting to deduct your armour bonus from them both first), then take the total from your LIFE points. If a guard is dead, don't add their damage rating. If you win a round, deduct the COMBAT points only from the guard you chose to attack. Remember to keep a note of how many rounds you have left for each guard.

FIRST GUARD

Rounds: 5   Damage: 2

SECOND GUARD

Rounds: 4   Damage: 3

YOU

If you win, turn to **326**.

If you lose, turn to **203**.

430

In desperation you find a rock and hammer it against the doors. The stone is so thick that the sound is almost lost to the wind and waves. You're about to give up when you hear a deep grinding noise, and the doors swing slowly inwards. Four armed men step out. You open your mouth, then realise there's not much to say.

You're taken down a tunnel that bends towards the mountain at the head of the inlet. It's lit by torches that flicker with green flame. Eventually you reach the dungeons, where you're stripped of your possessions and pushed inside a cell.

Turn to **301**.

431

The Lonely Isle looms on the horizon. You put the telescope to your eye and see grey cliffs scarred by deep clefts in the rock. Birds wheel and dive as the heavy sea dashes itself against... The telescope shakes in your hand. What was that? You thought you saw something move beneath the surface. Something large. You scan the waves but the low sun makes it hard to be sure.

You call towards Heston at the helm.

"Did you see that? I thought I saw something off the... Heston?"

His eyes are wide and his mouth hangs open. He points. A shadow falls across the deck as a great tentacle snakes into the sky. It must be five times the width of the mast. Its suckers twitch horribly and all around the ship more tentacles break through the waves. A vast mouth rises like a cavern filled with dripping stalactites, and a tongue emerges and hovers above the bow of the ship.

You hear a thin, high voice.

"Another one? So soon? The Lonely Isle seems poorly named."

There's a small figure growing from the end of the sea monster's tongue. He leans down to pick a piece of seaweed from the monster's tooth, then clears his throat politely.

"Good evening. My name is Pustula, and I represent the sea demon Gucifer. May I enquire who approaches the Lonely Isle? Your name and place of habitation only, if you please. We are not interested by rank or personal history."

If you want to tell this bizarre figure your name, turn to **229**.

If you want to lie, turn to **33**.

432

The 'arm' you're clinging to bends beneath your weight until you're face to face with the lifeless lure. With the last of your strength you fumble for the sleeping potion, pull the stopper out with your teeth, and pour. All the time, the clammy lure is slipping from your grasp. The creature gives a great sigh and its mouth starts to close. But too late! With a despairing cry you plunge into the foul pit.

Delete the SLEEPING POTION from your LOG BOOK,
then turn to **197**.

433

The beast pounces and pins you to the ground. You close your eyes, expecting this to be your lonely end. But suddenly the weight lifts from your chest. The strange mutant sits at your feet and whines sadly. Then it slinks off into the gloom. You scramble to your feet and run towards the city.

Turn to **348**.

434

You throw yourself backwards as something swishes so close by that you feel its cold breath on your cheek. A man curses and steps into the light, a mace hanging loose in his hand. You scrabble away, but he follows you into the street. Then another man emerges. And another...

Turn to **36**.

435

After leaving the Cat and Coracle, you retrace your steps from the night before. A guard watches you closely as you emerge from The Tangles, and you nod in his direction. He doesn't nod back, but lets you pass unhindered.

If you'd like to visit the market straight away, turn to **331**.

If you would first like to report your attempted kidnapping to the City Guard, turn to **200**.

If you'd like to go back to the workshop, to see if Old Joe has returned, turn to **377**.

STEP-BY-STEP COMBAT EXAMPLE

GUARD

Rounds: 5   Damage: 3

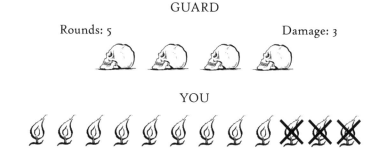

YOU

You have nine Life points, so before you start, you cross out three of the flames to make nine. You also have leather armour, which reduces the guard's attack by one Life point.

Round one

You choose 9+ and roll a 7. Your attack was unsuccessful. The guard attempts to inflict 3 Life points of damage on you, but your armour reduces it to 2 Life points.

GUARD

Rounds: 5   Damage: 3

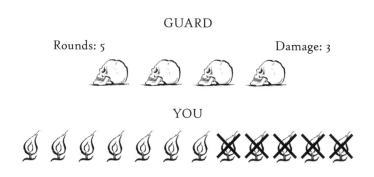

YOU

Round two

You choose 7+ and roll a 10. Your attack was successful. You deduct
1 Combat point for a 7+ roll.

GUARD

Rounds: 5   Damage: 3

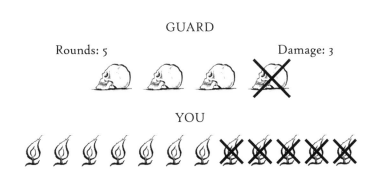

YOU

Round three

You choose 9+ and roll a 5. Your attack was unsuccessful. The guard
attempts to inflict 3 Life points of damage on you, but your armour
reduces it to 2 Life points.

GUARD

Rounds: 5   Damage: 3

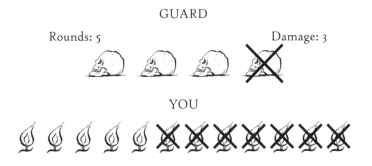

YOU

Round four

You only have two rounds left, so decide to roll for 9+ again. This time, you roll a 9. Your attack was successful. You deduct 3 Combat points for a 9+ roll. Your opponent has been defeated, and you can turn to the Victory paragraph.

GUARD

Rounds: 5   Damage: 3

YOU